Communications in Computer and Information Science   1615

More information about this series at https://link.springer.com/bookseries/7899

Dayang Norhayati A. Jawawi ·
Imran Sarwar Bajwa · Rafaqut Kazmi (Eds.)

Engineering Software for Modern Challenges

First International Conference, ESMoC 2021
Johor, Malaysia, October 20–21, 2021
Revised Selected Papers

Springer

Editors
Dayang Norhayati A. Jawawi 🄳
University of Technology Malaysia
Johor Bahru, Malaysia

Imran Sarwar Bajwa 🄳
Islamia University of Bahawalpur
Bahawalpur, Pakistan

Rafaqut Kazmi
Islamia University of Bahawalpur
Bahawalpur, Pakistan

ISSN 1865-0929   ISSN 1865-0937 (electronic)
Communications in Computer and Information Science
ISBN 978-3-031-19967-7   ISBN 978-3-031-19968-4 (eBook)
https://doi.org/10.1007/978-3-031-19968-4

This Springer imprint is published by the registered company Springer Nature Switzerland AG
The registered company address is: Gewerbestrasse 11, 6330 Cham, Switzerland

Preface

The present book collates accepted papers of the First International Conference on Engineering Software for Modern Challenges (ESMoC 2021), held in Johor, Malaysia, during October 20–21, 2021, and organized and hosted by the Islamia University of Bahawalpur and Universiti Teknologi Malaysia as a joint venture. The conference was sponsored by the Islamia University of Bahawalpur, Pakistan.

ESMoC 2021 received 167 submissions from authors in 13 different countries. After a single-blind review process, with each submission receiving at least 3 reviews, only 17 were accepted as full papers based on the classifications provided by the Program Committee, resulting in an acceptance rate of 11%. The selected papers come from researchers based in several countries including Malaysia, Australia, and Pakistan. The highly diversified audience gave us the opportunity to achieve a good level of understanding of the mutual needs, requirements, and technical means available in this field of research.

The selected papers reflect state-of-the-art research in different domains and applications of artificial intelligence and highlight the benefits of intelligent and smart systems in these domains and applications. They are organized into topical sections on software engineering, intelligent systems, and software quality. The high-quality standards of research presented will be maintained and reinforced at ESMoC 2023, to be held at the University of Greenwich, UK, and in future editions of this conference.

ESMOC 2021 also included five plenary keynote lectures given by Pooyan Jamshidi (University of South Carolina, USA), Dayang Norhayati A. Jawawi (Universiti Teknologi Malaysia, Malaysia), Shaohua Wan (Zhongnan University of Economics and Law, China), Shabana Ramzan (GSCWU, Pakistan), and Rab Nawaz (COMSATS University Islamabad, Pakistan). We would like to express our appreciation to all of them and in particular to those who took the time to contribute a paper to this book.

On behalf of the conference Organizing Committee, we would like to thank all participants. First of all, the authors, whose high-quality work is the essence of the conference., and the members of the Program Committee, who helped us with their eminent expertise in reviewing and selecting the quality papers for this book. As we know, organizing an international conference requires the effort of many individuals. We wish to thank also all the members of our Organizing Committee, whose work and commitment were invaluable.

The proceedings editors wish to thank the dedicated Program Committee members and all the other reviewers for their contributions. We also thank Springer for their trust and for publishing the proceedings of ESMoC 2021.

March 2022

Dayang Norhayati A. Jawawi
Imran Sarwar Bajwa
Rafaqut Kazmi

Organization

General Co-chairs

Dayang Norhayati A. Jawawi   University of Technology Malaysia, Malaysia
Imran Sarwar Bajwa   Islamia University of Bahawalpur, Pakistan
M. Asif Naeem   FAST-National University, Islamabad, Pakistan

Program Co-chairs

Imran Ghani   Indiana University of Pennsylvania, USA
Rafaqat Kazmi   Islamia University of Bahawalpur, Pakistan
Fairouz Kamareddine   Heriot-Watt University, UK

Organizing Committee

Dayang Norhayati A. Jawawi   University of Technology Malaysia, Malaysia
Rafaqat Kazmi   Islamia University of Bahawalpur, Pakistan
Sule Yildirim Yayilgan   NTNU, Norway
Ali H. Sodhro   University of Lyon 2, France
M. Taimoor Khan   University of Greenwich, UK
Irfan Hyder   Institute of Business Management, Pakistan
Riaz ul Amin   University of Okara, Pakistan
Noreen Jamil   FAST-National University, Islamabad, Pakistan

Program Committee

Adel Al-Jumaily   University of Technology Sydney, Australia
Adina Florea   University Politehnica of Bucharest, Romania
Adriano V. Werhli   Universidade Federal do Rio Grande, Brazil
Agostino Poggi   Università degli Studi di Parma, Italy
Ales Zamuda   University of Maribor, Slovenia
Ali H. Sodhro   University of Lyon 2, France
Alexander Gelbukh   National Polytechnic Institute, Mexico
Anand Nayyar   Duy Tan University, Vietnam
António Luís Lopes   Instituto Universitário de Lisboa, Portugal
Anna Helena Reali Costa   University of São Paulo, São Paulo, Brazil
Alvaro Rubio-Largo   Universidade NOVA de Lisboa, Portugal
Asif Baba   Tuskegee University, USA

Auxiliar Pedro Quaresma	University of Coimbra, Portugal
Aurora Ramírez	University of Córdoba, Spain
Barbara Ongaro	Liceo Alessandro Greppi, Italy
Bahram Amini	Foulad Institute of Technology, Iran
Bernard Moulin	Université Laval, Canada
Bujor Pavaloiu	Universitatea Politehnica din București, Romania
Carl James Debono	University of Malta, Malta
Carlos Filipe da Silva Portela	University of Minho, Portugal
Costin Badica	University of Craiova, Romania
Cyril de Runz	Université de Reims Champagne-Ardenne, France
Di Wu	North Dakota State University, USA
Dion Goh Hoe Lian	Nanyang Technological University, Singapore
Dong W. Kim	Inha Technical College, South Korea
Elias Kyriakides	KIOS Research Center, Cyprus
Fairouze Kammurdinne	Heriot-Watt University, UK
Farshad Fotouhi	Wayne State University, USA
Francesca Alessandra Lisi	Università degli Studi di Bari Aldo Moro, Italy
Gianluca Reali	University of Perugia, Italy
Gianluigi Ferrari	Università degli Studi di Parma, Italy
Giuseppe Boccignone	University of Milan, Italy
Grigore Stamatescu	Politehnica University of Bucharest, Romania
Hichem Omrani	Luxembourg Institute of Socio-Economic Research, Luxembourg
Hazart Ali	COMSATS University Islambabad, Abbottabad, Pakistan
Honghao Gao	Shanghai University, China
Isabel de la Torre Díez	University of Valladolid, Spain
Jan Platos	VŠB-Technical University of Ostrava, Czech Republic
Jamal Bentahar	Concordia University, USA
Janusz Wielki	Politechnika Opolska, Poland
Jolanta Mizera-Pietraszko	Wroclaw University of Technology, Poland
José Carlos Martins Fonseca	University of Coimbra, Portugal
José Moreira	Universidade de Aveiro, Portugal
José Fonesca	IPG- Politécnico da Guarda, Portugal
José Torres	Universidade Fernando Pessoa, Portugal
Juan Carlos Nieves	Umeå universitet, Sweden
Juha Röning	University of Oulu, Finland
Jurek Z. Sasiadek	Carleton University, Canada
Kiran Raja	Norwegian University of Science and Technology, Norway
Khurram Shehzad	University of Punjab, Lahore

Luis Fernandez Luque	Salumedia Labs, Spain
Luis Iribarne	University of Almería, Spain
Luis Jimenez Linares	Escuela Superior de Informática, Spain
Luis Rodríguez Benítez	Universidad de Castilla-La Mancha, Spain
Mariachiara Puviani	Università degli Studi di Modena e Reggio Emilia, Italy
Marko Hölbl	University of Maribor, Slovenia
Maxime Morge	Université de Lille, France
M. R. Spruit	Universiteit Utrecht, The Netherlands
Muhammed Cinsdikici	ComVIS Lab, Turkey
Marcin Pietron	AGH University of Science and Technology, Poland
Maria C. Nicoletti	Federal University of São Carlos, Brazil
Marjan Mernik	University of Maribor, Slovenia
Monireh Ebrahimi	Wright State University, USA
Natalia Bilici	Université du Luxembourg, Luxembourg
Pavel Skrabanek	Brno University of Technology, Czech Republic
Pedro Quaresma	University of Coimbra, Portugal
Preben Hansen	Swedish Institute of Computer Science, Sweden
Rafaqut Kazmi	Islamia University Bahawalpur, Pakistan
Ramoni Lasisi	Virginia Military Institute, USA
Rashid Ali	Yeungnam University, South Korea
Raymond Wong	University of New South Wales, Australia
Riaz-ul-Amin	Islamia University Bahawalpur, Pakistan
Ricardo Campos	Instituto Politécnico de Tomar, Portugal
Rodríguez García Daniel	Autonomous University of Barcelona, Spain
Roslina Binti Salleh	Universiti Teknologi Malaysia, Malaysia
Samir B. Belhaouri	Hamad Bin Khalifa University, Qatar
Silvia Parusheva	University of Economics - Varna, Bulgaria
Shamsul Islam	Edith Cowan University, Australia
Stefan Schulz	Medical University of Graz, Austria
Tara Yahya	University of Kurdistan Hewler, Iraq
Tatjana Sibalija	Belgrade Metropolitan University, Serbia
Thepchai Supnithi	Sirindhorn International Institute of Technology, Thailand
Thierry Badard	Université Laval, Canada
Tomislav Stipancic	University of Zagreb, Croatia
Václav Snášel	VSB-Technical University of Ostrava, Czech Republic
Weronika T. Adrian	University of Calabria, Italy
Yap Bee Wah	Universiti Teknologi MARA, Malaysia
Zbynek Raida	Brno University of Technology, Czech Republic

Invited Speakers

Pooyan Jamshidi	University of South Carolina, USA
Dayang Norhayati Jawawi	University of Technology Malaysia, Malaysia
Shaohua Wan	Zhongnan University of Economics and Law, China
Shabana Ramzan	GSCWU, Pakistan
Rab Nawaz	COMSATS University Islamabad, Pakistan

Contents

Software Quality

Software Engineering

Detection and Recognition of Software Design Patterns Based on Machine Learning Techniques: A Big Step Towards Software Design Re-usability

Shehzad Latif[1]($\boxtimes$), Muhammad Mukhtar Qureshi[2], and Mazhar Mehmmod[3]

[1] University of Management and Technology, Lahore, Pakistan
shehzadch49@yahoo.com
[2] University of South Asia, Lahore, Pakistan
[3] University of Agriculture Faisalabad, Faisalabad, Pakistan

Abstract. Design Patterns are techniques in software designing for addressing the frequently occurred issues in a relevant context. Understanding the design patterns used in the design helps to dive deeper into the design. Hence, mapping the design pattern is very necessary and valuable for Software designers to extract important information during the re-engineering process. Along with the detection of design patterns, it is also desired to recognize the design pattern from the source code. In this paper we presented an approach for design pattern detection and recognition using a machine learning techniques and metrics based training dataset.

Keywords: Software design patterns · Machine learning · Design pattern recognition · Reverse engineering · Design pattern detection

1 Introduction

A reverse engineering is the area of software engineering that is getting significant importance for the evolution and maintenance of software system [1, 2]. A main goal of this field is to get the portrayal of the system at higher level of abstraction and to detect the basic elements of the inspected system by using its structural details. Restructuring, updating and maintenance will be get simplified by retrieving the intelligible details of the system and the structure can also be perceived as a collection of organized modules rather than as a single unit. By taking these modules in consideration, design patterns can be detected [3].

In software engineering research domain design patterns have attracted the clear focus of researchers during past few years, as design patterns convey valuable information and have a strong impact on the design quality [4]. In addition, these can be utilized in a software system as a core component for improved implementation and its documentation. The key issues are the search, selection, use, verification and detection of design pattern [5–8]. *Searching* the design patterns means collecting the knowledge of current design patterns whereas, *selecting* the design patterns means picking a design

© Springer Nature Switzerland AG 2022
D. N. A. Jawawi et al. (Eds.): ESMoC 2021, CCIS 1615, pp. 3–15, 2022.
https://doi.org/10.1007/978-3-031-19968-4_1

pattern from a collection of available design patterns [6]. The *use* of design patterns is a method of implementing and integrating design patterns in the process of software development [8]. Moreover, *verifying* the design patterns and *detecting* the design patterns are crucial steps involved in the process of reverse engineering. They can significantly help in understanding the entire system. *Verifying* the design pattern means analyzing that the implantation done is as per its specifications or not whereas, *detecting* the design patterns means detecting the design elements in the source code [7].

In this research, our main focus was on design pattern detection and recognition problem because in reverse engineering process design patterns can provide significant information about the design to the designers [11]. The designer can use this information to develop a better understanding about the system. The core goal of pattern recognition is to correctly identify the design patterns which may enhance the scalability, modification, interpretation, replication, reconfiguration and recognition of the system [9]. Design patterns are valuable in acquiring information about the design problems of the system under observation [10].

Design patterns are commonly expressed using UML (Unified Modeling Language) which presents different models for implementation. These models are ambiguous causing uncertainties during system development. There is variety of notations for modeling is available for the study of pattern based detection of system design. The characterization of software design pattern is occurred in beginning phases of SDLC. Detection of patterns in software design is considered to be very valuable because it helps in scalability, modification, interpretation, replication and recognition by implementing effective techniques of reverse engineering. Recognition of design pattern is a most significant approach of software reverse engineering, which is affected the most from false positive and false negative problems [11]. Due to which accuracy of design pattern recognition got affected. This research proposes a method using which these problems can be solved. Our method transforms the whole procedure of recognition to a learning process. We identified instances in source code by using methods of supervised learning. *Decision Tree (DT)* and *Layer Recurrent Neural Network (LRNN)* techniques are applied in our methodology for the detection and recognition process. We considered *Adapter and Abstract Factory Design Patterns* for the process of identification. The suggested methodology is focused on supervised learning that utilizes data set dependent on object-oriented metrics.

The remaining paper is arranged as: Sect. 2 is the description of related works whereas; Sect. 3 is the proposed method. Section 4 is discussion and after which is the conclusion and future work.

2   Related Work

Detection is the most prominent problem in research area of Design Patterns [12]. The key features of the design pattern detection approaches are given in Fig. 1. On the basis of features approaches of design pattern detection are divided into two main categories which are "Behavioral Approaches and Structural Approaches".

2.1 Structural Approaches

Structural approaches describes the inter relationships of classes along with the identification of fundamental properties associated with the structure of design patterns for example attributes, functionalities, inheritance and its types, polymorphism and its types etc.) [11].

2.2 Behavioral Approaches

The core focus of behavioral approaches are to retrieve the information about the behavioral aspects of design patterns which help positively and significantly in the detection of those design patterns which are alike in structure [13]. *Furthermore these approaches are divided into more sub categories which are Semantic approaches and Syntactic approaches.*

2.2.1 Syntactic Approaches

The approaches in which we focus on the external features along with the structure of programming languages are known as Syntactic Approaches.

2.2.2 Semantic Approaches

The approaches in which we consider the meaning are categorized as Semantic Approaches [14].

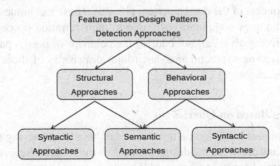

Fig. 1. Features based categorization of design pattern detection approaches

2.3 Techniques of Design Pattern Detection

According to the literature review we have categorized the available design patterns techniques into following categories as shown in Fig. 2.

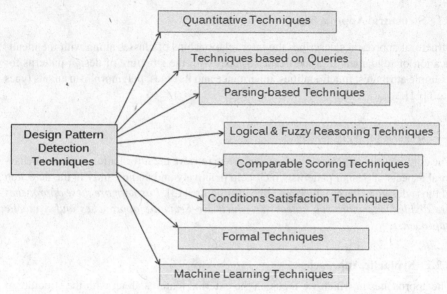

Fig. 2. Design pattern detection techniques

2.3.1 Quantitative Techniques

Quantitative techniques consider class-level features for metrics (for example counting the number of class relationships, data members and member functions) and afterwards use various methods to compare the calculated results with the predicted results which are based on the concept of the design pattern [15–20]. These techniques are considered to as efficient techniques computationally due to their filtration process. Approaches based on quantitative analysis do not address the behavior of design patterns as; these approaches are based on syntactic analysis. Major drawbacks of these techniques are interactivity and precision.

2.3.2 Techniques Based on Queries

Query based techniques are based on queries of database for retrieving the information of design patterns and detecting the design patterns on the basis of these retrieved queries [21–24]. These query-based approaches address the semantic aspects of the design patterns [24–26]. Major drawback of these techniques is its limitation to the query based information ignoring the other description which can provide some other details about the design patterns.

2.3.3 Logical and Fuzzy Reasoning Techniques

Reason techniques are divided into two main categories Logical Reasoning Techniques and Fuzzy Reasoning Techniques. In logical reasoning technique, the criteria for pattern detection are identified first then the actual detection of design pattern is made by using methods like backtracking. Its drawback is accuracy [33–35]. In a fuzzy reasoning technique, patterns of design are considered as fuzzy nets that represents standards for the detection of mini-structures identical to the design patterns. Its drawback is its high false positive rate and its dependency on understanding of the users [36].

2.3.4 Techniques Based on Parsing

These techniques for pattern detection mostly trace the syntax of visual language to its underlying graphical presentation for design patterns detection by utilizing the mechanism of parsing. Such methods are highly accurate but they are restricted to their own systematic variation [11, 47].

2.3.5 Comparable Scoring Techniques

Comparable scoring techniques describes the spatial details of the software design under observation and the sample design patterns to find resemblance between them [11, 27, 28]. The major drawback of these techniques is their accuracy issue in distinguishing design patterns which are similar in structure. Hence, such techniques are augmented with the techniques of behavioral analysis [29–32].

2.3.6 Conditions Satisfaction Techniques

These techniques for design pattern detection changes the issue related to detection of design pattern to issue of conditions satisfaction first and then define the elements of design as a specification structure where operations are expressed as variables and links between these operations are considered as conditions among these variables. The drawback of these techniques is their rate of precision and complexity whereas positive aspect is their high recall rate [37–39].

2.3.7 Formal Techniques

Formal techniques for design pattern detection are based on mathematical and logical approaches. These techniques are more expressive in nature but unfortunately these techniques have less precision as comparative to other pattern detection techniques. The major drawback of formal techniques is large computation and complexity. It is observed that these techniques are not that much successful when detecting the design patterns having a greater number of classes [40–46].

2.3.8 Machine Learning Techniques

Machine learning techniques are the most effective techniques which are used for the detection and recognition of design patterns. These techniques are basically seen as supplementary techniques to enhance the effect of structural techniques [20]. The main positive aspects of using the machine learning technique are their accuracy and effectiveness.

2.4   Design Pattern Detection Based on Machine Learning Approaches

Gueheneuc et al. [48] have proposed a mechanism for reducing the search scope of design patterns and created a repository of recognized cases known as library of design patterns. Moreover, for the recognition of classes performing specific tasks they have used machine learning approaches. Ferenc et al. [49] also detected and recognized Adapter and Strategy design patterns by using machine learning techniques like decision tree and back propagation neural network. Uchiyama et al. [50] also used back propagation mechanism of machine learning as well as software metrics for the detection of software design patterns. Alhusain et al. [51] have detected the pattern in their proposed work by using Artificial Neural Network (ANN) which is a machine learning approach. They have used different tools of pattern detection for creating their dataset and generated the features based input metrics by applying feature selection approach. Chihada et al. [20] have used supervised learning approach. They have implemented support vector machine to identify collection of design patterns. Di Martino [52] used Web Ontology Language for identifying and recognizing the design patterns. Gupta et al. [53] considered Normalized Cross Correlation for the detection of design patterns.

3   Proposed Technique

Our proposed technique is based on two steps which are i) Creation of Training Dataset and ii) Software Design Pattern Recognition.

3.1   Creation of Training Dataset

The process of creating training dataset involves four sub processes:

a.   Defining Software Design Patterns.
b.   Identifying Patterns Participants.
c.   Creating Feature Vectors by using Object Oriented Metrics.
d.   Pre-Processing of dataset.

Defining Software Design Patterns: Define the design patterns by considering its layout components for example problem and its solution, application and similar patterns etc. We can understand the meanings of software design patterns by analyzing its structural and behavioral aspects as determined by the Design Specialists.

Identifying Patterns Participants: Group of classes is known as Design Patterns. In a system based on design patterns these classes plays a particular and significant role. During pattern recognition each class require its unique identification. In our technique we use two types of Design patterns which are: *Abstract Factory Pattern and Adapter Factory Pattern*. Participants of Abstract Factory are *Abstract Factory-Abstract Product, Concrete Factory-Concrete* Product where as participants of Adapter Factory *are Adapter, adaptee and the target*. Moreover, function permutations can be reduced by eliminating those classes which do not perform any significant roles (Fig. 3).

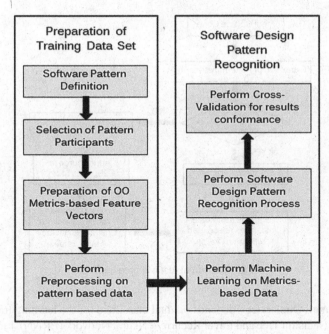

Fig. 3. Proposed model for software design pattern recognition

Creating Feature Vectors by Using Object Oriented Metrics: By utilizing different techniques of design patterns recognition like comparable scoring, web of patterns we create a feature vectors based on Object oriented metrics. Preparation of dataset dependent on metrics is shown in Fig. 4. Open source software code is taken as an input for various tools of pattern detection. Meanwhile, to retrieve desired classes based on metrics source code is also provided to JBuilder tools. Nominee instances based on metrics are analyzed against pattern instances retrieved from the detection tools. Hence, vectors based on feature are produced that involve values of metrics in a single row of all participant patterns.

Pre-processing of Dataset: Prior to learning process, preprocessing of the dataset based on metrics is done. In this step the complete size 219×269 dataset is divided into size 219×268 input dataset and size 219×1 aim dataset. The entire dataset is split into 80% and 20% dataset ratio, where 80% of the dataset is being used for the process of learning and the rest 20% dataset is being used for evaluation and analysis.

3.2 Software Design Pattern Recognition

To recognize design patterns binary classifiers are learned during this stage. It examines the formation of pattern participants and checks their availability in source code. Recognition of Software Design Pattern involves three sub stages which are as follows: Training Stage, Recognition Stage and Cross Validation Stage.

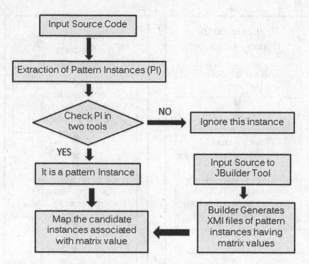

Fig. 4. Training dataset preparation

Training Stage: Our strategy depends on dual classifiers for the learning/training process, such as Decision Tree and Layer Recurrent Neural Network (LRNN). Layer Recurrent Neural Network (LRNN) in comparison to Feed Forward Neural Network (FFNN) utilizes its internal memory to conduct a number of inputs. One of the key reasons to support Layer Recurrent Neural Network (LRNN) is its repetitive nature. Decision Tree is also known as statistical model for the classification of vectors of input features based on goal values. It enables to return to the fragmentation of training data.

Recognition Stage: The structure of participant in patterns which are accessible in dataset used for training are tested with trained participants in design patterns during the identification of design pattern. Decision Tree and Layer Recurrent Neural Network (LRNN) are utilized in training datasets in this technique. Five-Fold cross validation is conducted to eliminate the under fitting and over fitting from the chosen ones.

Cross Validation Stage: Ultimately, validation for model conformance has been carried out using pattern description provided by pattern experts along with the retrieved results from the entire design pattern recognition process.

4 Results

To perform various experimentations we have used JHotDraw which is openly available for the recognition of design patterns. It has 160 Adapter Pattern instances and 59 Abstract Pattern instances. To measure the accuracy of the proposed technique we consider three factors which are (Accuracy (Precision), Recall and Harmonic Mean of Accuracy (Precision) and Recall (F-Measure) which are given below as:

$$Precision = \frac{\sum_{i=1}^{NDP} TPi}{\sum_{i=1}^{NDP} TPi + FPi}$$

$$Recall = \frac{\sum_{i=1}^{NDP} TPi}{\sum_{i=1}^{NDP} TPi + FNi}$$

$$F\text{-measure} = \frac{2 \times Precision \times Recall}{Precision + Recall}$$

NDP represent total number of design pattern instances. Total design patterns which are used in training datasets and are recognized by the classifiers are classified as True Positive (TP) whereas, those patterns not used in training process of dataset and still they are recognized by the classifiers are classified as False Negative (FN).

Accuracy results for Adapter Design pattern and Abstract design pattern are retrieved by using dual classifiers (i–e Decision Tree and LRNN). As shown below (Figs. 5 and 6):

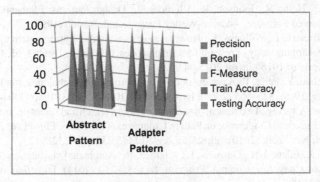

Fig. 5. LRNN based accuracy results

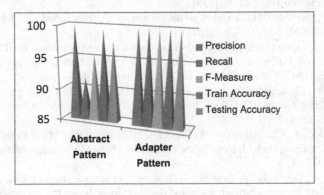

Fig. 6. Decision tree based accuracy results

5   Conclusion

Design pattern recognition is achieved by using Decision Tree and Layer Recurrent Neural Network. In our technique recognition of Design Pattern is performed by using

Adapter & Abstract Factory Design patterns. Experimentation is performed on JHot-Draw. We have achieved high accuracy by using preprocessing technique which reduces the number of pattern participants. The main goal we have achieved by using the machine learning process in our proposed technique is quality recognition of software design patterns.

References

1. Chikofsky, E.J.: Reverse engineering and design recovery: a taxonomy. IEEE Softw. **7**, 13–17 (1990)
2. Müller, H.A., Jahnke, J.H., Smith, D.B., Storey, M.A., Tilley, S.R., Wong, K.: Reverse engineering: a roadmap. In: Proceedings of the Conference on the Future of Software Engineering, ICSE, pp. 47–60. ACM, Limerick (2000)
3. Gamma, E., Helm, R., Johnson, R., Vlissides, J.: Design Patterns: Elements of Reusable Object-Oriented Software. Addison-Wesley Professional, Boston (1995)
4. Riaz, M., Breaux, T., Williams, L.: How have we evaluated software pattern application? A systematic mapping study of research design practices. Inf. Softw. Technol. **65**, 14–38 (2015). https://doi.org/10.1016/j.infsof.2015.04.002
5. Dong, J., Zhao, Y., Peng, T.: A review of design pattern mining techniques. Int. J. Softw. Eng. Knowl. Eng. **19**(6), 823–855 (2009). https://doi.org/10.1142/S021819400900443X
6. Birukou, A.: A survey of existing approaches for pattern search and selection. In: Proceedings of the 15th European Conference on Pattern Languagesof Programs, EuroPLoP 2010, pp. 2:1–2:13. ACM, New York (2010). https://doi.org/10.1145/2328909.2328912
7. Nicholson, J., Eden, A.H., Gasparis, E., Kazman, R.: Automated verification of design patterns: a case study. Sci. Comput. Program. **80**, 211–222 (2014). https://doi.org/10.1016/j.scico.2013.05.007
8. Eden, A.H., Gil, J., Yehudai, A.: Automating the application of design patterns. J. Object Oriented Program. **10**(2), 44–46 (1997)
9. Rasool, G., Streitfdert, D.: A survey on design pattern recovery techniques. Int. J. Comput. Sci. Issues (IJCSI) **8**(2), 251–260 (2011)
10. Priya, R.K.: A survey: design pattern detection approaches with metrics. In: IEEE National Conference on Emerging Trends in New & Renewable Energy Sources and Energy Management (NCET NRES EM), pp. 22–26 (December 2014)
11. Tsantalis, N., Chatzigeorgiou, A., Stephanides, G., Halkidis, S.T.: Design pattern detection using similarity scoring. IEEE Trans. Softw. Eng. **32**(11), 896–909 (2006). https://doi.org/10.1109/TSE.2006.112
12. Ampatzoglou, A., Charalampidou, S., Stamelos, I.: Research state of the art on GoF design patterns: a mapping study. J. Syst. Softw. **86**(7), 1945–1964 (2013). https://doi.org/10.1016/j.jss.2013.03.063
13. De Lucia, A., Deufemia, V., Gravino, C., Risi, M.: An eclipse plug-in for the detection of design pattern instances through static and dynamic analysis. In: Proceedings of the IEEE International Conference on Software Maintenance, pp. 1–6 (2010). https://doi.org/10.1109/ICSM.2010.5609707
14. Turbak, F.A., Gifford, D.K.: Design Concepts in Programming Languages. The MIT Press, Cambridge (2008)
15. Antoniol, G., Fiutem, R., Cristoforetti, L.: Design pattern recovery in object oriented software. In: Proceedings of the 6th International Workshop on Program Comprehension, pp. 153–160 (1998). https://doi.org/10.1109/WPC.1998.693342

16. Guéhéneuc, Y.-G., Sahraoui, H., Zaidi, F.: Fingerprinting design patterns. In: Proceedings of the 11th Working Conference on Reverse Engineering, pp. 172–181 (2004). https://doi.org/10.1109/WCRE.2004.21
17. Paakki, J., Karhinen, A., Gustafsson, J., Nenonen, L., Verkamo, A.I.: Software metrics by architectural pattern mining. In: Proceedings of the International Conference on Software: Theory and Practice (16th IFIP World Computer Congress), pp. 325–332 (2000)
18. Von Detten, M., Becker, S.: Combining clustering and pattern detection for the reengineering of component-based software systems. In: Proceedings of the Joint ACM SIGSOFT Conference – QoSA and ACM SIGSOFT Symposium – ISARCS on Quality of Software Architectures – QoSA and Architecting Critical Systems – ISARCS, pp. 23–32 (2011). https://doi.org/10.1145/2000259.2000265
19. Issaoui, I., Bouassida, N., Ben-Abdallah, H.: Using metric-based filtering to improve design pattern detection approaches. Innov. Syst. Softw. Eng. 11(1), 39–53 (2015). https://doi.org/10.1007/s11334-014-0241-3
20. Chihada, A., Jalili, S., Hasheminejad, S.M.H., Zangooei, M.H.: Source code and design conformance, design pattern detection from source code by classification approach. Appl. Soft Comput. 26, 357–367 (2015). https://doi.org/10.1016/j.asoc.2014.10.027
21. Rasool, G., Philippow, I., Mäder, P.: Design pattern recovery based on annotations. Adv. Eng. Softw. 41(4), 519–526 (2010). https://doi.org/10.1016/j.advengsoft.2009.10.014
22. Vokác, M.: An efficient tool for recovering design patterns from c++ code. J. Object Technol. 5(1), 139–157 (2006). https://doi.org/10.5381/jot.2006.5.1.a6
23. Rasool, G., Mäder, P.: Flexible design pattern detection based on feature types. In: Proceedings of the 26th IEEE/ACM International Conference on Automated Software Engineering, pp. 243–252 (2011). https://doi.org/10.1109/ASE.2011.6100060
24. Alnusair, A., Zhao, T., Yan, G.: Rule-based detection of design patterns in program code. Int. J. Softw. Tools Technol. Transfer 16(3), 315–334 (2013). https://doi.org/10.1007/s10009-013-0292-z
25. Thongrak, M., Vatanawood, W.: Detection of design pattern in class diagram using ontology. In: Proceedings of the International Computer Science and Engineering Conference, pp. 97–102 (2014). https://doi.org/10.1109/ICSEC.2014.6978176
26. Ren, W., Zhao, W.: An observer design-pattern detection technique. In: Proceedings of the IEEE International Conference on Computer Science and Automation Engineering, vol. 3, pp. 544–547 (2012). https://doi.org/10.1109/CSAE.2012.6273011
27. Dong, J., Sun, Y., Zhao, Y.: Design pattern detection by template matching. In: Proceedings of the ACM Symposium on Applied Computing, SAC 2008, pp. 765–769 (2008). https://doi.org/10.1145/1363686.1363864
28. Yu, D., Ge, J., Wu, W.: Detection of design pattern instances based on graph isomorphism. In: Proceedings of the 4th IEEE International Conference on Software Engineering and Service Science (ICSESS), pp. 874–877 (2013). https://doi.org/10.1109/ICSESS.2013.6615444
29. Dong, J., Zhao, Y., Sun, Y.: A matrix-based approach to recovering design patterns. IEEE Trans. Syst. Man Cybern. Part A: Syst. Hum. 39(6), 1271–1282 (2009). https://doi.org/10.1109/TSMCA.2009.2028012
30. Dong, J., Lad, D., Zhao, Y.: Dp-miner: design pattern discovery using matrix. In: Proceedings of the 14th Annual IEEE International Conference and Workshops on Engineering of Computer-Based Systems, pp. 371–380 (2007). https://doi.org/10.1109/ECBS.2007.33
31. Yu, D., Zhang, Y., Chen, Z.: A comprehensive approach to the recovery of design pattern instances based on sub-patterns and method signatures. J. Syst. Softw. 103, 1–16 (2015). https://doi.org/10.1016/j.jss.2015.01.019
32. Bernardi, M.L., Cimitile, M., Lucca, G.A.D.: Design pattern detection using a dsl-driven graph matching approach. J. Softw.: Evol. Process 26(12), 1233–1266 (2014). https://doi.org/10.1002/smr.1674

33. Kramer, C., Prechelt, L.: Design recovery by automated search for structural design patterns in object-oriented software. In: Proceedings of the Third Working Conference on Reverse Engineering, pp. 208–215 (1996). https://doi.org/10.1109/WCRE.1996.558905

34. Wuyts, R.: Declarative reasoning about the structure of object-oriented systems. In: Proceedings of the Conference on Technology of Object-Oriented Languages, pp. 112–124 (1998). https://doi.org/10.1109/TOOLS.1998.711007

35. Hayashi, S., Katada, J., Sakamoto, R., Kobayashi, T., Saeki, M.: Design pattern detection by using meta patterns. IEICE Trans. Inf. Syst. **E91-D**(4), 933–944 (2008). https://doi.org/10.1093/ietisy/e91-d.4.933

36. Niere, J., Schafer, W., Wadsack, J., Wendehals, L., Welsh, J.: Towards pattern based design recovery. In: Proceedings of the 24rd International Conference on Software Engineering, pp. 338–348 (2002). https://doi.org/10.1145/581380.581382

37. Guéhéneuc, Y.-G., Jussien, N.: Using explanations for design-patterns identification. In: Proceedings of the 1st IJCAI Workshop on Modeling and Solving Problems with Constraints, pp. 57–64 (2001). https://doi.org/10.1.1.150.4976

38. Albin-Amiot, H., Cointe, P., Guéhéneuc, Y.G., Jussien, N.: Instantiating and detecting design patterns: putting bits and pieces together. In: Proceedings of the 16th Annual International Conference on Automated Software Engineering, pp. 166–173 (2001). https://doi.org/10.1109/ASE.2001.989802

39. Guéhéneuc, Y.-G., Antoniol, G.: Demima: a multilayered approach for design pattern identification. IEEE Trans. Softw. Eng. **34**(5), 667–684 (2008). https://doi.org/10.1109/TSE.2008.48

40. Zhu, H., Bayley, I., Shan, L., Amphlett, R.: Tool support for design pattern recognition at model level. In: Proceedings of the 33rd Annual IEEE International Computer Software and Applications Conference, vol. 1, pp. 228–233 (2009). https://doi.org/10.1109/COMPSAC.2009.37

41. Wierda, A., Dortmans, E., Somers, L.: Pattern detection in object-oriented source code. In: Filipe, J., Shishkov, B., Helfert, M., Maciaszek, L.A. (eds.) ENASE/ICSOFT -2007. CCIS, vol. 22, pp. 141–158. Springer, Heidelberg (2008). https://doi.org/10.1007/978-3-540-88655-6_11

42. Mens, K., Tourwé, T.: Delving source code with formal concept analysis. Comput. Lang. Syst. Struct. **31**(3–4), 183–197 (2005). https://doi.org/10.1016/j.cl.2004.11.004

43. Tonella, P., Antoniol, G.: Object oriented design pattern inference. In: Proceedings of the IEEE International Conference on Software Maintenance, pp. 230–238 (1999). https://doi.org/10.1109/ICSM.1999.792619

44. Beyer, D., Lewerentz, C.: Crocopat: efficient pattern analysis in object oriented programs. In: Proceedings of the 11th IEEE International Workshop on Program Comprehension, pp. 294–295 (2003). https://doi.org/10.1109/WPC.2003.1199220

45. Smith, J., Stotts, D.: Spqr: flexible automated design pattern extraction from source code. In: Proceedings of the 18th IEEE International Conference on Automated Software Engineering, pp. 215–224 (2003). https://doi.org/10.1109/ASE.2003.1240309

46. Blewitt, A., Bundy, A., Stark, I.: Automatic verification of design patterns in java. In: Proceedings of the 20th IEEE/ACM International Conference on Automated Software Engineering, ASE 2005, pp. 224–232 (2005). https://doi.org/10.1145/1101908.1101943

47. Costagliola, G., De Lucia, A., Deufemia, V., Gravino, C., Risi, M.: Design pattern recovery by visual language parsing. In: Proceedings of the 9th European Conference on Software Maintenance and Reengineering, pp. 102–111 (2005). https://doi.org/10.1109/CSMR.2005.23

48. Gueheneuc, Y.-G., Sahraoui, H., Zaidi, F.: Fingerprinting design patterns. In: Proceedings of 11th Working Conference on Reverse Engineering, pp. 172–181. IEEE (2004)

49. Ferenc, R., Beszedes, A., Fülöp, L., Lele, J.: Design pattern mining enhanced by machine learning. In: Proceedings of the 21st IEEE International Conference on Software Maintenance, ICSM 2005, pp. 295–304. IEEE (2005)
50. Uchiyama, S., Washizaki, H., Fukazawa, Y., Kubo, A.: Design pattern detection using software metrics and machine learning. In: Joint 1st International Workshop on Model-Driven Software Migration, MDSM 2011 and the 5th International Workshop on Software Quality and Maintainability, SQM 2011-Workshops at the 15th European Conf. on Software Maintenance and Reengineering, CSMR 2011 (2011)
51. Alhusain, S., Coupland, S., John, R., Kavanagh, M.: Towards machine learning based design pattern recognition. In: 2013 13th UK Workshop on Computational Intelligence (UKCI), pp. 244–251. IEEE (2013)
52. Di Martino, B., Esposito, A.: A rule-based procedure for automatic recognition of design patterns in uml diagrams. Softw.: Pract. Exp. **46**, 983–1007 (2015)
53. Gupta, M., Pande, A., Singh Rao, R., Tripathi, A.: Design pattern detection by normalized cross correlation. In: 2010 International Conference on Methods and Models in Computer Science (ICM2CS), pp. 81–84. IEEE (2010)

Improving Traceability Using Blockchain and Internet of Things (IoT) in the Food Supply Chain

Muhammad Talal[1(✉)], Rafaqut Kazmi[1], Shahrukh[2], Gulraiz Javaid Joyia[1], and Tehmina Naz[3]

[1] Department of Software Engineering, The Islamia University of Bahawalpur, Bahawalpur, Pakistan
muh.talal@hotmail.com
[2] Department of Software Engineering, Superior University Gold Campus, Lahore, Pakistan
[3] National College of Business Administration and Economics, Bahawalpur, Pakistan

Abstract. In recent years, food traceability has become one of the emerging applications of Blockchain to strengthen the aspects of anticounterfeiting and quality control. This paper intends to suggest a methodology to improve traceability and transparency in food production and supply chain using Blockchain and the Internet of Things (IoT). Typical methods of the supply chain have loopholes, which are misused by antisocial groups to distribute unhygienic substandard food products. Blockchain technology guarantees the source of origin to a customer and enables traceability, tracking, and transparency which assists to increase accountability in the food production industry by confirming customer safety and protection, developing confidence, and enhancing the quality of service.

Keywords: Blockchain · Food production · Supply chain · IoT edge · Transparency · Traceability

1 Introduction

The worldwide supply chain market has grown over $13 billion in 2017 and is projected to expand beyond $19 billion by 2021 with Software as a Service (SaaS) increased sales potential [1]. The lack of accountability and knowledge sharing in the supply chain and delays in data collection impacting every phase of a logistics network. Moreover, product identification and traceability cannot be accomplished decently due to the fragmented and different structures of traditional Supply Chain Management (SCM), which the market is unable to tackle.

The primary obligation of the food production industry is to provide customers hygienic and safe food products. The main issue to the credibility of the food industry is the uncontrolled circulation of counterfeit food merchandise. In order to attain the social cause of hygienic, nutritious, and safe food products, it is important to provide a stable supply chain network there should be a mechanism for 'tracking and tracking' each product from the assembly line to a retail store (PoS) on the market [2] (Fig. 1).

D. N. A. Jawawi et al. (Eds.): ESMoC 2021, CCIS 1615, pp. 16–25, 2022.
https://doi.org/10.1007/978-3-031-19968-4_2

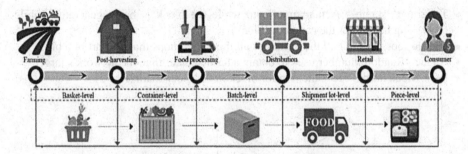

Fig. 1. Traditional food supply chain system

'Tracking' involves knowing at a certain given time the accurate physical position of a Food product within the supply chain. 'Traceability' is called the ability to track down the prior shape, packaging, site, period, and type of storage. As per the WHO definition of counterfeit "Product or device that is deliberately and fraudulently mislabelled with respect to identity and/or source".

In order to supply the quality product and stop entering the counterfeit product in the market, the capability to trace and track the whole supply chain is of the utmost importance. An effective food industry ecosystem usually consists of raw food suppliers, research facilities that facilitate the production process of hygienic and safe food products, regulatory approvals, industrial units, granaries, distribution channels, wholesalers, retailers, and consumers [3]. Every player should contribute essential data points to be tracked during the product's life cycle. For processing the information, we gather it must be stored safely and protected from any attempt of alteration. For example, information on the sourcing of raw materials, serial numbers, transmitting routes, storage areas, expiry dates of products, etc., should be traceable and kept accurately. Blockchain, started from Bitcoin, is an implementation of an append-only ledger. It holds completely traceable and immutable data, which transform data along with supply chain e.g. product inventory and distribution statistics. Blockchain technology' will enable supply chain for the food industry to have a reliable trace and track capability. This is accomplished by making sure that the food items could be tracked back to the source of origin of each and every ingredient at the point of sale. Thus, the completeness of the 'track and trace' loop is closed.

2 Securing Food Production Supply Chain Data Using Blockchain

Blockchain is a time-stamped collection of static digital records that can increase traceability, authenticity, ownership details, and anti-counterfeiting of current supply chains [4]. Blockchain comprises of data (records or transactions) registered in 'blocks' that are connected to establish a "chain of blocks" [5]. Every individual block in the Blockchain comprises of metadata in the block header, and a block having data.

Usually, the header section of the block contains the following metadata:

- Version Number – To make updates to the Software

- Time mark/stamp - Actual timestamp while the block is being generated (while processing begins for the candidate block)
- Merkle root - hash of all the hashes of all the transactions that are part of a block
- Nonce - Random number used to obtain a hash smaller than the network's target
- Prior Block hash – focus the to prior block in the blockchain (Fig. 2).

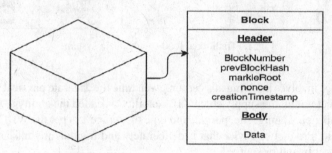

Fig. 2. Structure of a block in blockchain

The Blockchain consists of linear series of blocks, linked to the regular intervals chain [6]. The data in the blocks is based on the Blockchain network, but in all Blockchain variants the time-mark, transaction, and hash exist. Every block includes the previous block's cryptographic hash. All hashes are automatically generated, which ensures that no information can be modified in the hash. In this scenario, every next block will enhance previous block verification and all Blockchain security. The more blocks making stronger and more secure. Blockchain [7]. This arrangement confirms that all the blocks are connected in chronological order, through the prior block being referenced by each block, and it makes it impossible to modify or alter any data without changing all succeeding blocks. Protection feature inherited in the blockchain will aid to increase the integrity of data of next-generation supply chain systems.

A supply chain to the food industry through the Internet of Things (IoT) edge devices allows innovative technologies to be applied to increase transparency. IoT Edge devices aggregate sensor data, such as RFIDs, QR code readers, measuring scales, thermostats, GPS, and so on to help automate the gathering, processing, and validation of data. These data will be placed in blocks that are sequentially linked (in time series) to the edge device and further this data will be transferred to the cloud [8]. For end-user application allows safe data exchange and potential investigation or auditing (Fig. 3).

By keeping the cloud storage infrastructure in Blockchain for the end-user applications allows safe data exchange and potential investigation or auditing. Sensor systems and IoT can ensure end-to-end coverage to the life cycle of the product at manufacturers, production plants, distribution networks, and point-of-sale. Traceability and accurate data allow for value-added services such as demand planning, stock control, emergency alert, and automatic alert for grocery refill. Such requirements will be covered in subsequent sections (Fig. 4).

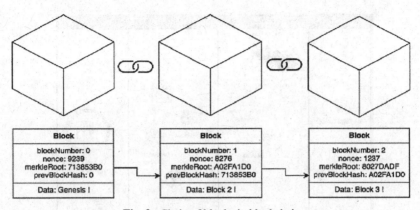

Fig. 3. Chain of blocks in blockchain

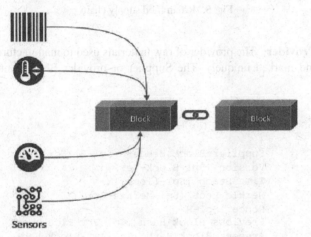

Fig. 4. Data from IoT devices to blockchain

3   Design Approach

The limitation in the current Supply chain is exhibited by the fact that the food companies do not have full control and visibility of the complex processes involved at each stage of the supply chain accompanying every stakeholder i.e. Manufacturer, Wholesaler, Distributor and Retailer, and End-user. In this research, basic conceptual design is mentioned that depicts the usage of IoT devices to formulate data acquisition, implementation of blockchain concepts aimed at complete data security, and the use of cloud technology for analysis of data, find loopholes and suggest comprehensive recommendations to rectify these shortcomings.

The fundamental design is primarily based on smart IoT devices linking the various stages of the supply chain, which are strongly linked via the intranet to a cloud backend. The functional approach and process involved at each stage and element of the supply chain system pertaining to Food companies are described below (Fig. 5).

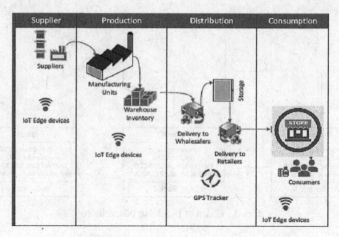

Fig. 5. IoT in food supply chain

Supplier or Provider: The provider of raw materials used to manufacture a food shall be labelled and marked uniquely. The Supplier or provider Block content could be comprised of:

```
Suppleer_Block (Spl-Blk):
        {
        Supplier_Block_Header (Spl-BlkHdr)
        Version (Spl-Block-Ver)
        Time_Stamp (Spl-Block_TM)
        Merkle_Root (Spl-Merkle-Rt)
        Nonce (Spl-N)
        Previous_Block_Hash (Spl-Prv-Block-Hsh)
        Present_Block_Hash (Spl-Pst-Block-Hsh)
        Supplier_Block_Data (Spl-Block-Data)
        {Spl-Trx1,…Spl-Trxn}
        }
```

Where the Vendor or Supplier transactions could be:

```
Suppliers_Transaction (Spl-Trx):
     {
     Version (Spl-Trx-Ver)
     Transaction_ID (Spl-Trx-ID)
     Supplier_Name (Name-Spl)
     ID (Spl-ID)
     Value_pairs (Spl-Val) - Supplier details
     Time_Stamp (Spl-Trx-TS)
     }
Raw_Item_Transaction (Raw-Itm-Trx):
     {
     Version (Raw-Itm-Trx-Ver)
     Transaction_ID (Raw-Itm-Trx-ID)
     Item (Name-item)
     ID (Spl-ID)
     Raw_Item_ID (Raw-Itm-ID)
     Name_item_Value_pairs (Spl-Val) - Raw Item details
     Time-Stamp (Spl-Trx-TS)
     }
```

Production: The industrial processing systems blend and refine the raw materials into a useable or edible product. With the following information, each unit of the assembly line will be distinctly identifiable:

1. Batch Details
2. Active item Materials
3. Amount/Numbers
4. Lifespan/Date of expiry.

The Production transaction contents may be:

```
Production_level_Transaction (Prod-Trx):
     {
     Version (Prod-Trx-Ver)
     Transaction_ID (Prod-Trx-ID)
     Industry_ID (Prod-Idy-ID)
      Name_Value_pairs (Val) - Provider, Site, and-
 Product Capacity
     Time_Stamp (Prod-Trx-TS)
     }
Batch_Transaction (Prod-Bth-Trx):
     {
     Version (Prod-Bth-Trx-Ver)
     Transaction_ID (Prod-Bth-Trx-ID)
     Industry_ID (Prod-Idy-ID)
     Batch_ID (Prod-Bth-ID)
     Name_Value_pairs (Val) - Product, Active Items
      Time_Stamp (Prod-Bth-Trx-TS)
      }

Unit_level_Transaction (Prod-Uni-Trx):
      {
      Version (Prod-Uni-Trx-Ver)
      Transaction_ID (Prod-Uni-Trx-ID)
      Batch_ID (Prod-Bth-ID)
      Unit_ID (Prod-Uni-ID)
      Name_Value_pairs (Val) - Distributor Node Trx,
Number, Lifespan, etc.,
      Time_Mark (Prod-Uni-Trx-TS)
      }
```

Distribution and Retailer: The units (lowest acceptable business entities) are stored and distributed at various nodes over different distribution routes. Distribution and retailers node transaction content could be:

```
Distributions_unit_Transaction (DistrUniTrx):
     {
      Version (Dist-Uni-Trx-Ver)
      Transaction_ID (Dist-Uni-Trx-ID)
      Distribution_Unit_ID (Dist-Uni-ID)
      Name_Value_pairs (Val) - Site, storage-capacity
      Time_Stamp (Dist-Uni-Trx-TM)
     }
```

Consumer: The units are linked to the buyers at the point of sale. The User Node content could be:

```
Consumer_Transaction (Cons-Trx):
      {
      Version (Cons-Trx-Ver)
      Transaction_ID (Cons-Trx-ID)
      Consumer_ID (Cons-ID)
      Time_Stamp (Cons-Trx-TS)
      }
```

4   Blockchain Benefits Over Other Information Security Systems

Common data protection mechanisms including network and hardware-level authenti-cation, role-based control on access, encryption, replication & data loss prevention, and abstraction techniques. Compared to conventional data storage approaches Blockchain has the following distinct advantages:

4.1   Decentralized Database

The Blockchain platform is decentralized and this is the biggest advantage. Working with a third party or with the central administrator is not required. Blockchain data does not follow the mechanism of central storage such as an application database, but as an alternative, it has a gold copy of the data available and where there are many nodes (intelligent edge devices) without any logical linking. Database that is decentralized increases the reliability of IoT applications' by eliminating one sole point of data storage failure. The benefit of having a gold copy is that if the node is under an attack it can be eliminated/erased and re-established with the latest blockchain 'gold copy'.

4.2   Data Immutable and Constantly Reconciled

A P2P network where all nodes have identical data, where the latest blocks are broad-casted, checked, and acknowledged through the nodes. Any alteration in the data of the chain is impossible to do without being identified and denied by all other nodes.

4.3   Consensus and Collaboration in Peer-to-Peer Network

Algorithms like Proof of Work (PoW) or Proof of Stake (Pos) are used to develop consensus and to kept data consistent between the nodes.

4.4   Securing the Network by the Authentic Users

The network nodes stay enabled, thus reducing the risk of attacking from the public influential node that can overwhelm the network.

4.5   Capable of Supporting Partial Node Chains

The network should be able to accommodate nodes that store limited chains locally, by taking into consideration 'last reconciled and conciliated block and adding further new blocks in the chain, as the IoT devices may be limited for storage. Each IoT device in such circumstances will take a different Blockchain and each new block will be connected to its particular the longest chain. Hence, the network sustains several blockchains.

5   Additional Value Adding Services from the Trace and Track System Through Blockchain

Traceability and accurate data allow value-added services which can benefit the food industry, retail stores, and consumers.

Production Plan: End-to-end data sources are available to enable managers of the company to forecast demand, plan product, run and maintenance events of production plant. This will lead to a reduction of the production unit operating costs.

Optimization of Inventories: Being aware of the product available downstream in the supply chain allows it possible for distributors and distribution stores to put orders with greater accuracy and precision. It will ensure buying and stocking of items 'just in time.'

Timely Alert/Notification: If a situation occurs in which a batch of Food products must be eliminated/recalled, it enables to monitor each individual item in the supply chain management system up to and including the end consumer. It would make it easier to take decisive measures and provide assurance that a tainted batch will not exist for the public/consumer.

Automated Alert for Grocery Refill: Consumer loyalty and satisfaction towards the brand or retailer will be improved by predictive delivery of grocery items.

Field Reviews and Feedback: Response from consumers, input from system operators and distributors will provide accurate data to production units for quality improvement and boost innovation (Fig. 6).

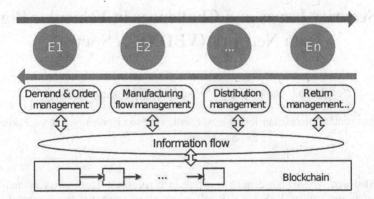

Fig. 6. Blockchain in supply chain management E1, E2...En represents the supply chain elements

6 Future Work

This paper presents an abstract framework and application of traceability based on blockchain. Many implementation aspects are yet to be studied. Reducing computing specifications for executing code of blockchain on IoT device having a minimal configuration and inherited data fault tolerance in-network and devices. Another study area would be lightweight protocols for network coordination and propagation.

References

1. Wu, H., Cao, J., Yang, Y., Tung, C.L., Jiang, S., Tang, B., et al.: Data management in supply chain using blockchain: challenges and a case study. In: 2019 28th International Conference on Computer Communication and Networks (ICCCN), pp. 1–8 (2019)
2. Shamsuzzoha, A., Ehrs, M., Addo-Tenkorang, R., Nguyen, D., Helo, P.T.: Performance evaluation of tracking and tracing for logistics operations. Int. J. Shipp. Transp. Logist. **5**, 31–54 (2013)
3. Koh, R., Schuster, E.W., Chackrabarti, I., Bellman, A.: Securing the pharmaceutical supply chain. White Paper, AutoID Labs, Massachusetts Institute of Technology, vol. 1, p. 19 (2003)
4. Malik, S., Dedeoglu, V., Kanhere, S.S., Jurdak, R.: TrustChain: trust management in blockchain and IoT supported supply chains. In: 2019 IEEE International Conference on Blockchain (Blockchain), pp. 184–193 (2019)
5. Miller, D.: Blockchain and the Internet of Things in the industrial sector. IT Prof. **20**, 15–18 (2018)
6. Bahga, A., Madisetti, V.K.: Blockchain platform for industrial Internet of Things. J. Softw. Eng. Appl. **9**, 533–546 (2016)
7. Fernández-Caramés, T.M., Fraga-Lamas, P.: A review on the use of blockchain for the Internet of Things. IEEE Access **6**, 32979–33001 (2018)
8. A. I. E. documentation: Azure IoT Edge documentation. https://docs.microsoft.com/enin/azure/iot-edge/

Security Issues and Challenges in Vehicular Big Data Network (VBDN): A Survey

Irshad Ahmed Sumra$^{(\boxtimes)}$ and Ahmad Naeem Akhtar

Department of Information Technology, Lahore Garrison University, Lahore, Pakistan
irshadahmed@lgu.edu.pk

Abstract. VANET is becoming more prominent network due to its safety and non-safety applications. V2V and V2R will generate huge amount of data in network. Big data technology is attractive and more challenges task for researcher to manage the data in next generation vehicular network. Evaluate the big data technologies in VANET and it is beneficial and useful to perm huge amount of computational data, provide better transportation system and gain exponential result. Vehicular communication network restrains the organized processing, wireless communication and sensing ability. The Big Data tools facilitate to gather the data, combination of different ways and handing out of data from heterogeneous services. So, in this paper, it provides the comprehensive survey on security issues and challenges in Vehicular Big Data Network (VBDN). Some big data technologies are useful to overcome the security issues of big data in VANET.

Keywords: Big data · Vehicle to vehicle (V2V) · Vehicle to roadside unit (V2R) · Vehicular Big Data Network (VBDN)

1 Introduction

VANET contain materialized considering that an electrifying explores and appliance area. Vehicular communication network restrains the organized processing, wireless communication and sensing ability. VANET produce the huge quantity of data for special functions like (increase the car speed, high mobility of node, location, expansion). In VANET rising form of communication comprise intra-vehicle, V2V and infrastructure essentials Vehicle to Infrastructure (V2I) and VANET is reflecting on an exceptional variety of MANET [1]. VANET drive is a foremost part in the direction of the recognition of intelligent transportation systems (ITS) [2]. The data exchange in excess of VANETs frequently plays an imperative function in traffic safety and very strict security necessities are to be accomplished. In VANET collect the useful information for the helping of drivers; make dictions to perfume the activities and sometime interrupt the information for predominantly in driver supporting systems. VANETs are measured significant outstanding to their enormous prospective and frequent relevance. VANETs not only present massive protection development but also much profitable prospect. Safety driving is one of the major events dynamic features of traffic protection, so there is an unambiguous and need is to be safer so VANET provide all the satisfaction capabilities to secure transportation management system (Fig. 1).

D. N. A. Jawawi et al. (Eds.): ESMoC 2021, CCIS 1615, pp. 26–35, 2022.
https://doi.org/10.1007/978-3-031-19968-4_3

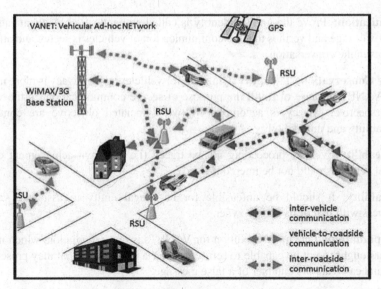

Fig. 1. VANET architecture [1]

The remaining paper is ordered in different sections. The Sect. 2, discuss the security requirements of VANET and in Sect. 3 briefly illustrate basic concept of big data network. The Sect. 4 describes the relationship of VANET with big data, vehicular big data network and combination of VANET with big data. Different type of VANET challenges and their solutions with Big Data also discuss in this section. Section 5 concludes the paper.

2 VANET Security Challenges

Security and privacy pay an important role to make the VANET superstitions, popular and unique all the transportation system. For this purpose, identify some security requirement to fulfill the privacy needs and provide secure wireless communication between the two vehicles [3]. Data transformation in secure manner and protect the attacker. In the case of accident provide the awareness to the drivers and helps to take any action such a ridicules situation. Security sight VANET determine be additional challenges. Actuality, every communication model has a special set of security requirements [4].

2.1 Security Requirements

This section contains the verification of requirement different communication system. Illustrate the communication system authenticate the requirements according to the security condition and fulfill the vehicle needs depending the situation.

Identification: Each entity encloses unique value and different to the other entity. Vehicular Identification contains number or VIN. Registration number demonstrates the identity certificate for each vehicle.

Authentication: Prove the unique identity is called authentication. Authentication is an approval stage and verifies that the communication of vehicles is secure and attacker interrupts in the conversation.

Privacy Conservation: Privacy is significant for vehicles. User privacy is more important in VANET because of fulfill the purpose of secure communication. In the vehicular perspective, privacy is accomplished two associated objective are contented untraceability and unlink ability.

Untraceability: Vehicle proceeding not be traced (i.e. different achievement of the identical vehicle should not be interconnected).

Unlinkability: It should be unfeasible for an illegal entity to associate vehicle uniqueness with that of its driver/owner.

Non-repudiation: One more condition for VANETs is non-repudiation, which means that users ought to not be capable to refuse transfer a message so that they preserve is follow and castigate in container of a false message.

Confidentiality: In group communication massage will only read authorize party So that secure communication built in both parties. Only group members read the information.

Availability: Each node is alert and active to send the information to the other node because this connectivity very important to the road safety this is vital a requirement to the security.

Trust: Trust is the key factor in V2V and V2R [5] and data integrity and correctness must be ensured in trust procedures. Straightforwardly data is important should not be modify so that trust is an important requirement for VANET communication.

2.2 VANET Security Challenges

To achieve the goals and secure communication it is necessary to accomplish the security challenges in this table show some security challenges. The penalty of a security violation in VANETs is serious and unsafe. The components of vehicular networks are given below [6].

- The driver: Driver plays vital role in the VANET safety because this entity takes the decisions.
- The vehicle: In VANET two types of vehicles 1) normal vehicles 2) malicious vehicles.
- Roadside unit (RSU): The Standard roadside units can illustrious the normal way.
- Third party: Trust is donated by the third party and all digital equivalents of stakeholders in a direct way in ITS.
- The Attacker: In VANET security, the attacker is one of the compromise entities that effect the network due to different types of attacks. There is different security mechanism to secure the communication and ensure the safety and non-safety applications deliver to end users.

Secure VANETs systems necessary are capable also to establish the dependability of drivers while preserve their privacy and detail description are given below [7].

Real Time Constraints: VANET achieve the real time constraints so, required the specific timing to deliver the massages. Achieve this goal use very fast cryptographic algorithm.

Data Reliability Obligation: Data consistency is important in VANET and avoids the unnecessary information because authenticate node execute the malicious.

Low Tolerance for Error: In Some procedures are scheduled based on1 possibility. VANET achieve the action in very short time.

Key Distribution: VANET use the key to send and receive the messages encrypts the message and after procedure complete decrypt the message that's why key distribution is an important procedure and perform the major challenge.

High Mobility: High mobility is required in VANET nodes are connected each other's and transfer the signals to communicate the other vehicle so very fast mobility level is required. VANET required less execution time.

Incentives: In vehicular networks, the prosperous ingesting will require incentives for vehicle manufacturers and users and the govt is a challenge to ensure the security in vehicular network.

Non-repudiation: In this procedure node cannot refuse but does not send the messages and signals. It's going to be crucial to work out the proper sequence in crash re-establishment.

Data Verification and Privacy: To preserve the integrity, regular bases check the verification and privacy is very essential characteristic in VANET.

2.3 Threats to Availability

Threat to the availability in VANET is given below [8].

Denial of Service (DoS): In this type of attack, it can be completed by an indoor, and or outdoor in the network, this attack is occurred when the network is unavailable to the valid users.

Broadcast Tampering: An insider attacker is carried out such kind of attack and it forward false safety messages into the vehicular network and such messages harm to the other users of the network.

Malware: This attack is frequently approved by insiders more than outsiders and when a firmware update is done it can be downloaded into the system.

Spamming: In vehicular network, there is no central management to control and monitor the activity of vehicle in network, so spam messages in VANET are more difficult to control and research work is in progress to solve such security issue in dynamic vehicular network.

Black Hole Attack: This attack is the cause of broadcasting messages and vehicles refusing to join in the network when the nodes slump the network than all communications and links had broken.

2.4 Threats to Authenticity

Threat to the authenticity in VANET is given below [9].

Masquerading: In such kind of attack, it is easier to catch out and in masquerading threat and attacker joins the network and the attacker possess as an acceptable vehicle in the network.

GPS Spoofing: GPS spoofing through the GPS satellite simulator creates the false location and move the vehicle wrong side to ensure that this location is right one. GPS satellites generated stronger the signals and secure the network.

Replay Attack: The attacker reinserts the communication packets and send to the other vehicle in network. It can poison a node's location table by repeating bacons in network.

Tunnelling Attack: The attackers swiftly insertion the false positioning data into the dedicated unit of the vehicle and derivation the vehicle to accept that the data received is authentic and action perform on this valid information.

Fake Position Attack (Sybil Attacks): In position Faking attackers can speedily modify their own position or that of other vehicles and unsecured communication link or channel can generate a blind spot produce extra individuality.in such kind of attack, it is even block vehicles from receiving and dispatch vital and reliable security messages.

Message Tampering: The attacker modifies and exchanged the message from V2V or RSU vehicular communication network.

2.5 Threats to Confidentiality

The confidentiality is one of the key security goals in vehicular network and passive attacks which are directly affect the user privacy in VANET [2].

2.6 Basic Concept of Big Data Network

Big data is defined as "an all-encompassing term for any collection of data sets so large and complex that it becomes difficult to process using traditional data processing applications". Big data has quickly residential into a hotspot topic and it magnetize great concentration from academia, industry, and governments. The growing of data day by day and very huge amount of data difficult to handle and processing, to fulfill this purpose to use databases but sometimes data complexity is too much increase traditional database not capable to handle this situation. So, control this situation introduce the big data. Big data is the collection of data sets which is huge and complex, generally size of the data is Petabyte and Exabyte [10]. It can observe the Big Data in different fields finance, business, banking, stock exchange and online purchasing. Big data provide many facilities to make the better organization and reduce the time cost other functional operation that's why this technique promote the business and many helpful to different fields such that banking, administration, education, analysis, data collection, storage, information extraction and cleaning. According to these definition two types of data divide two categories: Physical world and human society in physical world achieve the data through the sensor scientific experiments and observation etc. and in human society like internet, health, finance, transportation.

Big Data issues and Challenges: Numerous issues will have to be deal with to imprison the full prospective of big data some vital issues discuss in given below [11, 12].

- Data Complexity: When big data solve the computational problems, they face the additional complex data entity. The intrinsic density of big data constructs it sensitive as well as complex variety, complex composition, and complex model.
- System complexity: Reduces the system complexity use the interactive computational system, validations, theories or beneficial algorithm.
- Security Sustain: Security plays the vital role to promote the big data and secure computational of data. Some security requirements are to be important.

5Vs of Big Data: The detail description of 5Vs are given below [13].

- Volume: Large amount of exponential growth convention in the volume of big data. Data is not containing just in the appearance of text data, but also in the structure of videos, music and huge image. So, enlargement of the database need to re-structure the architecture and assemble the application organize to the big data.
- Velocity: In velocity suitable reaction necessities in it and according to the situation timely reaction is more important also required quick response.
- Variety: Different variety of data is available in different formats like structure, structure semi structure data capability big data handle and manage the data in various varieties also emerging the data easily.
- Variability: Variability is one of the key features of 5Vs and Variability is to increase the varieties of data and data flows can be highly inconsistent with periodic peaks in network.

- Value: Value shows the value of data and its relationship with other data sources and it can be able to collect monetarize and analyze the data (Fig. 2).

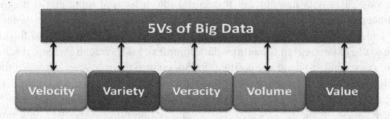

Fig. 2. Characterization of multi-V model of big data

3 VANET with Big Data

The theory of VANET has materialize as a well-organized method to recover and manage the transportation systems, improve the security and provide facilitate to deal with organize the traffic problems find the better solution.

Vehicular Sensor Network (VSN): The VSN is basically collections of networks that send and receive the signals through the nodes these nodes are interconnected each other and capture the signals the purpose of data gathering for different devices, sensors, cell phones perfume this activity increase the complexity of VANET [15]. The VANET will generate large amounts of data and detail description of these types of data are given below:

Solve these problems which face that modern society now a days. Big Data tools facilitate to gather the data, combination of different ways and handing out of data from heterogeneous services. Big Data technologies to VANET, one can increase helpful approaching from an enormous quantity of functional data, to develop traffic organize procedure. Big data utilize various tools like map reduce, HDFS, HADOOP [14]. The VANET is reflecting on an exceptional variety of MANET and VANET produce the huge quantity of data for special functions like (increase the car speed, high mobility of node, location, expansion). Merge these two technologies VANET and BIG DATA are very beneficial to the future and fulfill the user needs, requirements and Structured.

1. Unstructured
2. Semi-structured
3. Mixed

3.1 VANET Challenge with Big Data

Numerous challenges in VANET can be deal with using Big Data solutions and method. Different type of data is available in VANET and big data face many challenges and to perform the tasks according to the user needs. Discuss VANET challenges in big data and find the solution different researchers.

Appropriate Filters to Extract Useful VANET Information: Big data retrieve the information use complementary tools for dictions making and analysis machine learning techniques. Filtering is basically reduce the problems so big data use the appropriate filter to manage and reduce the data broadness when data is so complex it's very difficult to stable but involve the big data section cover its complexity and make them very useful to the future use [16].

Removal of Redundant Information in the Collected Data: Other case is to handle the huge amount of data use the redundant process basically big data remove all the redundant steps and efficient retrieve so, in VANET we try to remove all the redundant form of data because its increase the complexity and problematic to coverage therefore we need develop and introduce the efficient system to like big data to easy coverage and solve VANET raw data issues.

Traffic Management Using Predictive Models: VANET faces the big issues related to traffic management data retrieve various sources (roads, cameras, sensors) use limited capabilities much difficult to control the VANET transportation system so, it's a challenge to process the fast data on the right time.

4 Secure Communication

The Secure communication is one of the biggest issues to the any technology, data coverage is important but secure data is most important to successful done the achievements VANET gather various types of data so increase the complexity and also increase the unsecure data, faces many security and privacy problems. Introduce some algorithms to identity and authenticity to secure communication. Big data can use the encryption keys to secure the communication one vehicle to another [18].

4.1 VANET Characterizes and Attribute of Big Data

It has tried to map some of these VANET characteristics to attributes of Big Data validate that VANET problems can be handle as Big Data issues and can be solved using methods of Big Data. The detail descriptions are given blew [17].

- Real time data: Need the large table to update and store the VANET data but VANET data automatically work. The volume part generates the different data sources in the real time.
- Variable network density: Variable network density depends upon the variable vehicular density. These vehicles are well-found different sensor devices and produce the various forms of data. The variety part of big data refers that the coming of data various ways such that structure and unstructured data.
- Highly Dynamic topology and Mobility modelling: In VANET node is referring to the vehicle's nodes. These nodes are connected to each other's and divide the large result into small chunks. These features of VANET justify the velocity and generate the very fast rate of data without rate of generation.

- Large Scale network and high computational ability: Many GPS increase the capacity of nodes very large-scale networks so; the value part of big data is very important that analysis the nodes behavior and decide.
- Anonymous addressee and potential support from Infrastructure: Identification of vehicles is most major requirement of vehicular infrastructure however the veracity part of big data related inevitability and reliability that ensure that data is secure and protect.

5   Conclusion

VANET generate the huge quantity of data for special functions like (increase the car speed, high mobility of node, location, expansion). The Data exchange in excess of VANETs frequently plays an imperative function in traffic safety and very strict security necessities are to be accomplished., big data has quickly residential into a hotspot topic that magnetize great concentration from academia, industry, and yet governments because growing of data day by day. The 5V's (Volume, Velocity, Variety, Variability) of big data are the attribute of big data and In this survey paper, discuss in detail the security issues and challenges in Vehicular Big Data Network (VBDN) and provides the detail description that use of some VANET technologies is to approve that which big data technologies is better for VANET. The illustrate the big data in VANET because data complexity is too much increase traditional database not capable to handle this situation, so introduce Vehicular Big Data Network (VBDN) to process the large amount of data.

References

1. Da Cunha, F.D., Boukerche, A., Villas, L., Viana, A.C., Loureiro, A.A.F.: Data communication in VANETs: a survey, challenges and applications (2014)
2. Contreras-Castillo, J., Zeadally, S., Guerrero, J.A.: Solving VANET Challenges with Big Data Solutions. University of Colima, Mexico, University of Kentucky, USA, University of Colima, Mexico (2016)
3. Bedi, P., Jindal, V.: Use of Big Data Technology in Vehicular Ad-hoc Networks (September 2014)
4. De Fuentes, J.M., González-Tablas, A.I., Ribagorda, A.: Overview of security issues in Vehicular Ad-hoc Networks (2011)
5. Zaidi, K., Rajarajan, M.: Vehicular internet: security & privacy challenges and opportunities. Future Internet 7(3), 257–275 (2015)
6. Mejri, M.N., Ben-Othman, J., Hamdi, M.: Survey on VANET security challenges and possible cryptographic solutions. Veh. Commun. 1(2), 53–66 (2014)
7. Toshniwal, R., Dastidar, K.G., Nath, A.: Big data security issues and challenges. Int. J. Innov. Res. Adv. Eng. (IJIRAE) 2(2), 15 (2015)
8. Mishra, R., Sharma, R.: Big data: opportunities and challenges. Int. J. Comput. Sci. Mob. Comput. 4(6), 27–35 (2015)
9. Jiang, H., Wang, K., Wang, Y., Gao, M., Zhang, Y.: Use of big data technology in vehicular ad-hoc networks. Energy Big Data: A Survey (March 2016)
10. Li, Z., Wang, Z., Chigan, C.: Security of vehicular adhoc networks. In: Wireless Technologies in Intelligent Transportation Systems, pp. 133–174. Nova Publishers (2011)

11. Zikopoulos, P.C., Eaton, C., deRoos, D., Deutsch, T., Lapis, G.: Understanding Big Data: Analytics for Enterprise Class Hadoop and Streaming Data. McGraw-Hill, United States of America (2012)

12. Ranjani, S.: Security threats on vehicular ad hoc networks (VANET): a review paper. In: National Conference on Recent Trends in Computer Science and Technology (NCRTCST) (2013)

13. Cardenas, A.A.: Top ten big data security and privacy challenges: security clouds alliance.org (November 2012)

14. Dean, J., Ghemawat, S.: MapReduce: simplified data processing on large clusters. Commun. ACM **51**, 107–113 (2008)

15. Lämmel, R.: Google's MapReduce programming model—revisited. Sci. Comput. Program. **70**(1), 1–30 (2008)

16. Sumra, I.A., Hasbullah, H.B., Ab Manan, J.lb.: User requirements model for vehicular ad hoc network applications. In: International Symposium on Information Technology 2010 (ITSim 2010), Malaysia (2010)

17. Sumra, I.A., Ahmad, I., Hasbullah, H., bin Ab Manan, J.: Behavior of attacker and some new possible attacks in Vehicular Ad hoc Network (VANET). In: 2011 3rd International Congress on Ultra Modern Telecommunications and Control Systems and Workshops (ICUMT), pp. 1–8 (October 2011)

18. Sumra, I.A., Hasbullah, H., Ab Manan, J., Iftikhar, M., Ahmad, I., Aalsalem, M.Y.: Trust levels in peer-to-peer (P2P) vehicular network. In: 11th International Conference on ITS Telecommunications (ITST), pp. 708–714. IEEE (2011)

Analysis of Web Monitoring Servers and Tools for Cloud Computing Services

Nadeem Sarwar[1]([⊠]) [iD], Junaid Nasir Qureshi[1], Tahir Iqbal[1], Haroon Abdul Waheed[2],
Muhammad Hammad Yasin[3], and Asma Irshad[4] [iD]

[1] Computer Science Department, Bahria University Lahore Campus, Lahore, Pakistan
Nadeem_srwr@yahoo.com, {JNqureshi.bulc,
tahir.iqbal}@bahria.edu.pk
[2] Department of Software Engineering, University of Central Punjab, Lahore, Pakistan
haroon.waheed@ucp.edu.pk
[3] Faculty of Computing, Riphah International University, Islamabad, Pakistan
Hammadyasin4699@gmail.com
[4] School of Biochemistry & Biotechnology, University of the Punjab, Lahore, Pakistan
asmairshad76@yahoo.com

Abstract. This research aims to find best cloud service monitoring tools and techniques according to trending parameters. The services of cloud computing are most popular services now a days. Many organizations are migrating to cloud technology in order to reduce the management's complications of resources. The effective monitoring methodologies should be implemented, to certify the Quality of Experience (QoE) and Quality of Services (QoS) of cloud computing services for end users. For this purpose, cloud services should be monitor and control using different tools and techniques. There are so many server-based or web-based monitoring tools are available. In this paper, analysis of different tools is based on their pricing, working efficiency, key features, platforms and environments in which they could be used. This paper also analyzes the cloud computing structure and investigates that which type of monitoring services are required at which level. This research paper shows that no monitoring tool is mature enough to fulfil all requirements and desires of clients. This research also interprets that which tool is recommended for which kind of platform and environment.

Keywords: Cloud computing · Network traffic · Monitoring tools · QoS (Quality of Services) · Matrices · Pipelines

1 Introduction

Cloud computing technology has become a famous and favorite technology for many organizations. That's why many organizations are drifting toward cloud technology to lessen the complexity of managerial tasks. Cloud services providers are working on the principle of 'pay as you go' so, all services should be monitor and measure carefully. To monitor cloud services and resources, cloud service providers are using different tools and techniques. These tools could be installed on both clients and vendors end. The main

© Springer Nature Switzerland AG 2022
D. N. A. Jawawi et al. (Eds.): ESMoC 2021, CCIS 1615, pp. 36–43, 2022.
https://doi.org/10.1007/978-3-031-19968-4_4

aim of monitoring tools is to monitor the functioning of resources and equipment. Monitoring tools are very beneficial to identify and prevent flaws in services and network of services. A good monitoring tool will provide great control over technology or services (which are provided by vendors) to examine QoS (Quality of Services), and performance [10, 11]. Monitoring system will also alert the user about defects and flaws of systems. Monitoring systems will enhance the performance of resources and services. Best monitoring systems' evaluation is based on of some parameters such as: identification of problems or errors, create an alert of errors, provide an interface to monitor or control usages of resources, create or maintain log and session files of resources usage, find ideal configurations and settings, monitor number of users and traffic etc. Cloud-based systems are may be comprising on broad range of software solutions and applications for examples: Internet of Thing (IoT). These systems should bear burden of resources, and huge volume of data that is used and generated by end-users. To overcome all these problems, traditional centralized cloud architecture is replaced by different modern decentralized cloud architecture.

1.1   Centralized Cloud Structure

Centralized cloud structure is a traditional structure. In centralized architecture, single and centralized server responds multiple clients. Server is responsible for provision of all resources that are requested from clients' end. Server will be compatible to handle all desired tasks. Centralized cloud computing is comprised on different layers shown in Fig. 1. Centralized cloud computing consists of datacenters. Datacenters may be provided by any third party. Centralized cloud can be used as long-term storage and for computational purposes. In centralized application may be composed of different modules and chunks. This framework may also serve different surveillance services using IoT devices. Now a days, services of Amazon, Microsoft and Alibaba etc. are based on centralized cloud architecture. Figure 1 shows centralized cloud structure [1, 8] and [9].

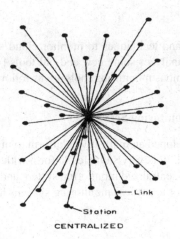

Fig. 1. Centralized Cloud Structure [3]

1.2 Decentralized Cloud Structure

In Decentralized cloud environment, systems and frameworks are distributed into different nodes. All nodes are capable to respond requests of services. Cloud Structure have not a single point of control. In this cloud computing structure, chance of failure of services get reduced because whole environment is distributed into different nodes. If one of computing nodes is not responding an appropriately other node will respond a request. In this environment stored data may be transparent and can be accessible by everyone. In today's world EOS, TRON and Ethereum are well known platform of decentralized cloud structure. Figure 2 demonstrates structure of decentralized cloud structure [2, 8] and [9].

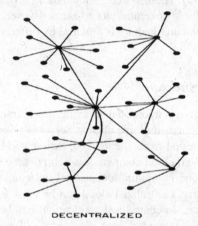

DECENTRALIZED

Fig. 2. Decentralized cloud structure [3]

2 Analysis

There are so many tools and techniques to monitor cloud services. To find best tool and technique this paper analyzes some new and old tools [4]. Introduction and some detailed information of famous monitoring tools are as followed (Table 1):

2.1 Anturis – Server Monitoring Services

Anturis Incorporation developed an innovative platform to monitor infrastructure internally and externally as well. It is very suitable platform with appropriate facilities such as scalability of resources, centralized monitoring system and reporting management. It also supports agent-based or agent-less monitoring systems [5].

2.2 AppOptics – Application Monitoring Services

It is a SaaS based application used for monitoring of applications' performances. It is developed by SolarWinds. It is deigned to face and solve different monitoring problems. It supports more than 150 integrations, distributed tracing, alerting pipelines and lots of libraries, plugins and frameworks such as Go, Node.js and Scala etc.

2.3 Datadog – Cloud Monitoring Services

Datadog is based on SaaS infrastructure developed by Datadog organization. It provides a platform to examine all endpoints of services. It provides several utilities such as: databases, servers, applications and user-friendly interface of infrastructure.

It gives a hybrid environment for Dev and Ops squads to done job collaboratively [6, 7].

2.4 Instrumental – Free Server Accounts

Instrumental is a platform that's monitor functioning of applications and servers. It provides free services up to 500 metrices. It is a best platform for instant visualization of resources, automated means of data collection and it can process millions of datapoints with in few seconds.

2.5 Tornimo – Real-Time Analytics and Monitoring Application

Tornimo is a cloud-based application powered by Codewise. Frontend of Tornimo is designed by Garafana dashboards and it is hosted by Amazon Web Services (AWS) cloud. It provides a graphite friendly environment. Users can easily install any monitoring tool in this application. It also reduces the data arrival delay.

2.6 Cisco Cloud Consumption Service

Cisco Cloud powered by Cisco systems. Consumption service cloud of Cisco provides an infrastructure which is quite efficient to find or identify cloud services and protect services or resources from different threats. Clients can get analytical reports of usages of cloud resources. It also serves in different ways such as security of cloud services and resources, hybrid IT environment and solution support.

2.7 CopperEgg – Cloud Monitor

CopperEgg is a services monitoring application developed by IDERA Software Solutions. It provides a tracking platform to track websites and cloud resources. It delivers fast and smart cloud services to monitor and optimize web servers. It gives a user-friendly interface which updates with in few seconds and retrieve all archived detailed information [8, 9].

2.8   Countly – Mobile Monitoring Platform

Countly is an innovative platform in the monitoring tools' universe. It offers mobile, desktop and web-based interfaces to monitor and analyze the metrices and datapoints of cloud resources. It provides numerous utilities on a single dashboard. It could be extendable via different plugins.

2.9   Munin – System and Networked Monitoring Application

Munin is a platform used for monitoring purposes and it is developed by Trac. It examines all the resources and generate a graphical report of all analyzed information and present these reports via web interface. It also enables extensions via different plugins with less efforts [12, 13].

2.10   Nagios – IT Management and Analytic Tool

Nagios is a versatile monitoring system. It provides a powerful and single platform for different operating systems including Windows and Linux. It also offers monitoring utilities for log servers, applications, SNMP-enabled systems and other networking servers.

2.11   Check MK – Hybrid Environment for IT Management

Check_MK is an extended version of Nagios monitoring system. It is best platform for networking, cloud and server monitoring. It also serves analytic services for database, storage and container servers.

2.12   Dynatrace – APM

Dynatrace is the emerging and leading monitoring tool in application performance management (APM) environment. It is based on artificial intelligence engines at the backend. It will deal with top to bottom managerial tasks using automatic algorithms smartly.

2.13   Oracle – Performance Monitoring Tool

Oracle performance monitoring tool is powered by Oracle incorporation. It offers a fusion environment to analyze and encounter the problems. It can troubleshoot many problems and errors with less effort.

2.14   LogicMonitor – Host-Based Network Monitoring

LogicMonitor offers monitoring services for cloud-based, virtual and physical systems. It also provides facility of fast deployment of SaaS-based monitoring structure. It is based on web console which have preconfigured databases, switches, routers and firewalls. It also generates SMS or email-based alerts for IT management [14].

Table 1. Information of famous Server monitoring tools

Sr#	Names	Features	Developer	Price $	Source
		☐ Network protocols.			
01	Anturis	☐ Server and websites moni-toring.	Anturis, Inc.	/mo.Starting from $10	https://anturis.com/
		• Reports and Alerts.			
		• Modern monitoring infrastructure.			
		$ 1,199			
02	AppOptics	☐ Seamless performance	SolarWinds	– $ 2,999 /yr.	https://www.appoptic s.com/
		analysis.			
		• Self-instrumented APM. ☐ State-based analysis.			
03	Check MK	☐ Event-based analysis.	Checkmk	$ 600 - $ 1200 /yr.	https://checkmk.com/
		• Customizable user interface.			
		• Hybrid Kubernetes monitoring.			
04	Cisco Cloud	☐ Easy managements of con-tainers and datasets.	CISCO, Inc.		m/ https://www.cisco.c o
		Flexible.			
		• Integrated platform for different cloud services.			
		• Design database models.			
05	CopperEgg	☐ Analyze database working.	Idera, Inc.	$ 1,996 - $ 2,156/ in-	https://www.idera.co
		• Prevent database from stallment.			m/ threats.
		Community Edition			
		• Mobile analytical platform. is Free. While,			
06	Countly	☐ Webcation.-based analytical appli-	Countly, Inc.	Enterprise Edition's	https://count.ly/
		• Easy installation of plugins. price is according to requirements.			
		• Visualization of perfor-			
07	Datadog	mance of resources.	Datadog, Inc.	$ 1 - $ 31 /mo.	https://www.datadogh q.com/
		• Graphical analysis of logs, metrices and traces.			
		• Generates alert for errors.			
		• Artificial intelligent plat-			
		form.		Dynatrace	

(continued)

Table 1. (*continued*)

08	Dynatrace	□ Preconfigured and automated environment.	software company.	$ 0.04 /hr.	https://www.dynatrace.com/

- Cloud monitoring platform.
- Support query languages.

09	Instrumental	□ User friendly design.	Instrumental, Inc.	$ 0.0034 metric /day.	https://instrumentalapp.com/

- Smart error alerts.
- Realtime cloud monitoring services.

10	LogicMonitor	□ Deals with management. configuration Flexible.	Inc.LogicMonitor, n	ration	itor.com https://www.logicmo/

- Enterprise and inhouse IT management.
- Monitoring of computer, databases and networks.

11	Munin	□ Offers all services on plug and play basis.	Munin, Org.	Free	http://munin-monitoring.org/

- Prebuilt graphical interface.
- Provides a virtual environment for different third parties.
- Offers a hybrid platform for

12	Nagios	different operating system. It also supports different networking protocols.	Nagios, Org.	$ 1995 - $ 6,495 (Limited – Unlimited edition.)	https://www.nagios.com/

- Provides resources to Dev and Ops team.
- Represent all application

13	Oracle	performance information on a single console.	Oracle, Org.	Flexible.	https://www.oracle.com/cloud/systems-management/application-performance-

- Identification of key errors monitoring.html

3 Conclusion

This paper concluded that cloud computing is a need of today's organizations and to monitor cloud services is also a crucial task. By the increase in use of cloud resources cloud monitoring is now becoming a quite mature and trending business. This trending business have few gaps and flaws which should be filled by using different effective techniques and services such as auditing of services, management of resources, support different platforms, fault management and 24/7 availability of services. This review paper also analyzed different trending and famous monitoring tools for different scenarios. We hope, this review paper would act as an effective reference paper for further researches in cloud community.

References

1. https://www.sciencedirect.com/science/article/pii/S016412121730256X#tbl0002
2. https://nakov.com/blog/2018/04/24/the-upcoming-decentralized-cloud-dpaas-decentralize dcomputing-db-storage-as-a-service/
3. https://www.softwareadvice.com/resources/it-org-structure-centralize-vs-decentralize/
4. https://haydenjames.io/50-top-server-monitoring-application-performance-monitoring-apm solutions/
5. https://anturis.com/
6. https://tornimo.io/?utm_source=haydenjames.io&utm_medium=banner&utm_campaign= influencers&utm_content=300x300#newsletter
7. https://www.oracle.com/cloud/systems-management/application-performance-monitoring. html
8. Bayat, M., Doostari, M., Rezaei, S.: A lightweight and efficient data sharing scheme for cloud computing. Int. J. Electron. Inf. Eng. **9**(2), 115–131 (2018)
9. Lee, K.: Comments on "Secure Data Sharing in Cloud Computing Using RevocableStorage Identity-Based Encryption." IEEE Trans. Cloud Comput. **8**(4), 1299–1300 (2020)
10. Sun, X., Wang, S., Xia, Y., Zheng, W.: Predictive-trend-aware composition of web services with time-varying quality-of-service. IEEE Access **8**, 1910–1921 (2019)
11. Bouraqia, K., Sabir, E., Sadik, M., Ladid, L.: Quality of experience for streaming services: measurements, challenges and insights. IEEE Access **8**, 13341–13361 (2020)
12. Mebarkia, K., Zsóka, Z.: Service traffic engineering: avoiding link overloads in service chains. J. Commun. Netw. **21**(1), 69–80 (2019)
13. Li, S., Wei, C., Yan, X., Ma, L., Chen, D., Wang, Y.: A deep adaptive traffic signal controller with long-term planning horizon and spatial-temporal state definition under dynamic traffic fluctuations. IEEE Access **8**, 37087–37104 (2020)
14. Cui, Z., Henrickson, K., Ke, R., Wang, Y.: Traffic graph convolutional recurrent network: a deep learning framework for network-scale traffic learning and forecasting. IEEE Trans. Intell. Transp. Syst. **21**(11), 4883489 (2019)

XSHM: Proposed Hybrid Process Modeling Technique from Scrum and XP for PSP and Medium Projects

Muhammad Irfan Malik[1], Muhammad Zafar Iqbal Karmani[2], Nadeem Sarwar[2]([⊠]) [iD],
Junaid Nasir[2], and Allah Ditta[3]

[1] Department of Computer Science, Virtual University of Pakistan, Lahore, Pakistan
MS170400529@vu.edu.pk

[2] Department of Computer Science, Bahria University Lahore Campus, Lahore, Pakistan
zafarkarmani6@gmail.com, Nadeem_srwr@yahoo.com,
Junaid.jans@gmail.com

[3] University of Education, Lahore, Pakistan
allahditta@ue.edu.pk

Abstract. In this paper I have tried to propose and new hybrid model of XP and Scrum already existing models and naming XSHM, It is a proposed model for agile software development industry. The proposed model is helpful for agile software development for the development of personal software process and medium software development projects. This model has the flexibility to adopt strong and useful features of both scrum and extreme programing models and skip or cutoff all the unsuitable and less affective modules of both model. This model may have Advantage and disadvantages by adopting this technique. I did so to make it clear for the people who are confused while choosing any modeling technique in some situations of agile development. I have not only discussed their working of XP and scrum in agile but also their advantages and disadvantages as well. After reading this paper, reader will be able, understand the working of both XP, scrum models in agile techniques, and be able to choose the XSHM in their useful situation. It will also clear the working and importance of software development of PSP and medium software projects using proposed model. I have tried my best to explain techniques used in XSHM in this paper so that reader may be able to use it and aware about its importance and choose the most suitable one for his situation.

Keywords: XSHM · Agile · XP · Scrum · Extreme programming · PSP

1 Introduction

Everyday's technology and methods of doing work are improved. It is due to rapid advancement and development of changing environment. Models are introduced in the number of ranges and every model has its own advantages. There is a gap to allow all models to apply on same project and got all advantages. It is a useful way to hybrid useful features from different systems and a low it to apply on new developing products to made it facilitated at maximum range. For such manners many systems are working

D. N. A. Jawawi et al. (Eds.): ESMoC 2021, CCIS 1615, pp. 44–52, 2022.
https://doi.org/10.1007/978-3-031-19968-4_5

as hybrid. One of most knows hybrid development system is Novel model. This work is proposed a simple and efficient workable hybrid model for agile software development for PSP and medium projects.

It is a proposed technique in which two existing models are hybrid to get a new hybrid model for the facilitation of industry. It is a useful way to reduce cost and time. It also helps to utilize resources in actual manners. Here it is introduced that useful phases of both models are inject in a new proposed model skeleton and give it a shape of a new model. As its hybrid of XP and Scrum models. It is named as XSHM (Fig. 1).

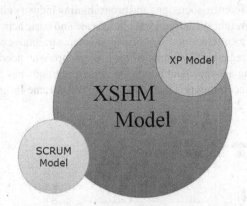

Fig. 1. Broad picture of XSHM proposed model

The above figure is the graphical representation of new Hybrid model. Which is adopting some portion of both Scrum Model and some portion of other XP model? It will be helpful for future agile software development of medium and small projects.

2   Literature Review

Programming improvement experiences the Skelton and right way. Deft models have gained popularity in recent decades due to their ease of use, adaptability, and suitability for displaying programming development needs. Numerous dexterous models like discussed below:

2.1   Extreme Programming

Programming businesses are continuously receiving the coordinated improvement practices of modified models, for example, Scrum or Extreme Programming (XP) or Rational Unified Process (RUP). Scrum and Extreme Programming (XP) are every now and again utilized deft models, though Rational Unified Process (RUP) is one well known great arrangement driven programming improvement procedure. Both deft and plan driven models have their own benefits and bad marks, for example, XP has great designing practices, group joint effort and then again feeble documentation, lacklustre showing in medium and enormous scale ventures. Scrum depends on venture the executives rehearse. RUP model has a few impediments, for example, unrealistic for little and quick paced ventures, inclination to be over planned, denounce fast changes in necessities. This examination paper dependent on proposes novel crossover structure XSR by joining qualities of Scrum, XP and RUP by smothering their constraints to deliver top notch programming.

2.2 Working of Extreme Programming

Extreme Programming (XP) is the most exceptionally embraced dexterous practice and broadly utilized in different associations and programming industry all through the world. XP is basic and lightweight spry strategy for little scale and basic activities. XP accept on essential five working codes/values are correspondence, straightforwardness, criticism, mental fortitude and regard. XP is intended for little groups who need to work in a quick and fast programming advancement condition, where prerequisites are changing every now and again and uncommonly. Detailed working of Extreme Programming is shown in the following Fig. 2.

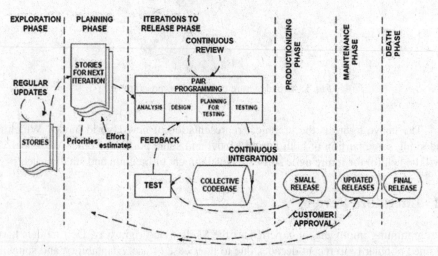

Fig. 2. Source (IJCST vol.8 3, 2017): life cycle of extreme programming model

XP is the useful software development programing model using for many of years ago in agile software development approach.

2.3 Working of Scrum Framework

Scrum is an experimental approach that incorporates adaptability and performance into the development process by relying on the hypotheses of process control [10, 11]. The three focuses of scrum are straightforwardness, analysis, and modification. Straightforwardness means that any step in the process that affects the result should be clear to all involved in product development. Examining involves keeping a close eye on the protocol in order to detect any unsuitable anomalies (Fig. 3).

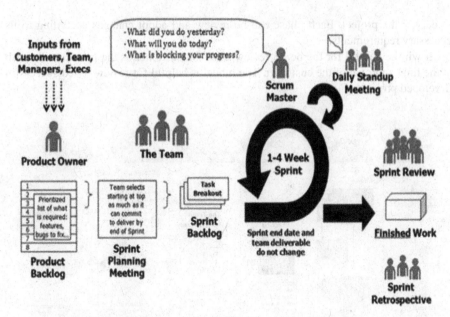

Fig. 3. Source (IJCST vol.8 3, 2017): life cycle of scrum framework

Scrum is a managed framework for agile software development it helps the management of software development like reviewing scheduling and actively participating in agile software development.

3 Proposed Model

The subject model use at its center for the proposed show. In any case, of agile software development the developers working on personal, small or medium size products can use a new proposed model. This model consists of the hybrid of both Scrum framework and XP model. The specific goal of this model is to get the useful features from both XP and Scrum and hybrid both of them in proposed model XSHM. It will be available for agile software developers to enhance their capabilities and skills from in the era of software development.

The model is separate out into six main phases associated with software development life cycle (SDLC). Adopted the requirement gathering techniques from the XP model. It is gathering requirements from team management and customers. There are backlogs created where it is planned for the working and distributions of tasks for next iteration. The responsibilities are divided at third phases and we named it as a Task Breakouts here every working member of the body will get responsibility to complete his responsible task in time with deliverables. Daily Meetings of 10 to 15 min will be the ensured that the working is properly managed and linearly doing according to its lifeline, In next phase it is Review the product and checking the working of the developed product, User comments are necessary for ideal changes for the next phase we get review and brief the customer about developed product, Final approval of owner is necessary at last phase to deploy the project. Each phase can be review and adopt changes according to its necessary requirements.

It will be helpful for the better review from the customer as the project will finish at the final approval of the customer. The model is helpful for review based successful developed projects (Fig. 4).

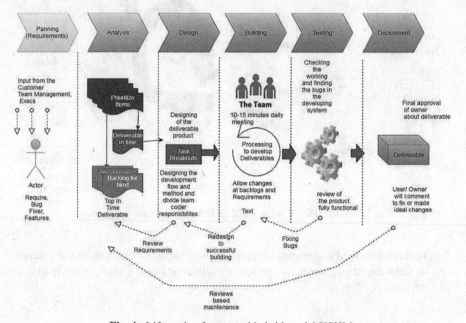

Fig. 4. Life cycle of proposed hybrid model XSHM

Each phase has its own responsibilities and working which is done in that specific phase. Phases of XSHM model are described in detail here.

3.1 Phases of XSHM

The scrum is a system, while XP is an engineering process. Both have advantages, which are described in this paper. Proposed the XSHM model, which is a hybrid model for agile practices that combines the XP and Scrum models (Scrum Hybrid model, XP).

Scrum has the best features of management, and XP has good engineering practices, as described in the paper. We developed a new model to help with the process by integrating Scrum management functionality with XP engineering process methods. Our proposed model (XSHM Model) will run in six phases of the SDLC (Software Development Life Cycle).

The following is a working outline of each process in the proposed integrated model:

Planning: In the planning step, our integrated proposed scheme XSHM receives feedback and gathers user requirements, as the model would collect data from the product's owner and we will forego the story-defined method for gathering requirements. Customers, Team management, and Execs provide this detail. It is the step of the model where data on requirements collection, features of emerging products, and bug fixes in the proposed model will be collected.

Analysis: Prioritized items must be chosen and production must begin on the basis of these prioritized products in this step of the XSHM Model. It should be noted about the deliverable products based on the requirements analysis. The deliverables can be divided into two categories. Time will begin to produce deliverables, while other deliverables will be held in backlogs to be created in order in future deliverables.

Design: The most crucial step of our proposed working model is this one. The XSHM Model is used to design the product which is deliverable product as well as the whole production flow. It is often used to delegate and separate the development roles of the final deliverables' sub-models. This model uses the XP creation techniques, but it lacks the scrum framework's short sprint cycles. It allows for improvements in sprint backlogs to be made here. The expert working team members made these improvements to the deliverables. If there are any concerns about the deliverables. The review process will run during the regular meeting and will be completed. This design phase will proceed to the construction phase.

Building: This is the final step of the deliverable product's creation, during which developers will create the designed modules within a set time frame. Every day, the team will meet to discuss what needs to be done and what is currently happening. What exactly is reaming? Since the team members meet on a regular basis, it's crucial to establish the specifications and backlogs allow for changes. If there are any additional/high-level problems that occur during the production of the deliverables. The design process is a reminder of the development problems.

Testing: This step of the XSHM ensures that the deliverables are developed/built successfully and that the system is working properly. If there is an error that is causing the device to malfunction or has the potential to do so in the future, it will be highlighted here. The building process is recalled in order to correct the bug and ensure the system's optimum functionality.

Deployment: This is the final stage of the developed framework, the XSHM Model. Only by successfully going through each phase can the product arrive in the form of deliverables in this phase. If the owner will leave a message here, I will make some ideal changes. The method will recall from the review step if it is important to his desire. On the other side, once the owner has given final approval to the user, it would be shipped and the agile iteration using this model will be completed. The final deliverable may be launched or linked, and work on the next deliverables begins.

3.2 Introduce ETVX in the Model

For the XSHM Model, here is the ETVX pattern explanatory model (Scrum Hybrid model, XP) (Tables 1 and 2).

Table 1. ETVX pattern for XSHM model (Scrum Hybrid, XP model)

Entry: Function of product ownership adaptation	Task: Prioritize the things on your list. Developing future deliverables	Exit: When the customer/product owner has given final approval to the deliverable
	Verification: Examining the high-priority item is practical	

Table 2. Details of each step of the XSHM model

1	2	3	4	5	6
Requirements from the product's owner	Timely deliverables	Mission separation	Processing in order to create deliverables	Analysis of the fully functional product	Owner's final approval is required for delivery

Entry: Only the product owner has the adaptation function according to the Scrum model.

Task: The tasks are to complete the creation of things that have been prioritised.

Verifications: The product verification will be confirmed by the testing validation process and the owners' comments on the product.

Exit: Exiting is possible after the customer/product owner has given final approval to the deliverable.

3.3 Advantages of XSHM

This form is superior to Scrum and XP. Since it is a combination of both models (XP and Scrum), it is focused on implementing features from both.

- This model is adaptable and follows the XP engineering approach, which is the best agile-based iterative and light-weight model of software development and engineering.
- It is lightweight, adaptable, and manageable throughout development; this quality distinguishes it from scrum.
- This suits XP engineering methods, so it has a well-developed Skelton development model.
- Since it collects information from a representative position of product ownership, it needs less time and energy than the XP model.
- It started the planning process by concentrating exclusively on the elements that were prioritized. The XP model lacks this functionality because it focuses on the next iteration, which is time consuming and results in late deliverables.

- This system is superior to scrum because it allows for improvements to sprint backlogs. It will take some time and effort, but it will reduce the difficulty of complete iterative deliverables in terms of time and expense.
- This method would save money on labour because in scrum, a scrum master is responsible for ensuring that the team follows the framework. Only regular meetings on the analysis of work will be held under this model.
- There isn't any test-driven growth in it.
- Unlike XP, there is no refactoring or collective ownership code.
- In this model, there is no need for continuous configuration.
- It will help the owner to design the product according to desired budget estimation.

4 Conclusion

Agile is the famous technique of software development. Software industry is a digital and manageable industry. This proposed module will have great impact in agile software developers. It will help them to achieve their milestones with efficient working and in time. The developer will have a good experience of practicing modules of both extreme programming model as well scrum framework. A new hybrid model has capabilities for further improvements in management and space for module injection if possibly available or introduced through future work. If there is best module even than any of its working modules. It can be replaced in future research working.

References

1. Pervez, M.T., Dogar, A.B.: Mapping formal methods to extreme programming (XP)–a futuristic approach. Int. J. Nat. Eng. Sci. **8**(3), 35–42 (2014)
2. Kobayashi, O., Kawabata, M., Sakai, M., Parkinson, E.: Analysis of the interaction between practices for introducing XP effectively. In: Proceedings of 28th International Conference on Software Engineering, pp. 544–550 (May 2006)
3. Deemer, P., Benefield, G., Larman, C., Vodde, B.: A lightweight guide to the theory and practice of scrum. Ver **2**, 2012 (2012)
4. Ahmad, G., Soomro, T.R., Brohi, M.N.: Agile methodologies: comparative study and future direction. Eur. Acad. Res. **1**, 3826–3841 (2014)
5. Khan, A.I., Qurashi, R.J., Khan, U.A.: A comprehensive study of commonly practiced heavy and light weight software methodologies. Int. J. Comput. Sci. Issues **8**(4), 441–450 (2011)
6. Qumer, A., Henderson-Sellers, B.: Comparative evaluation of XP and Scrum using the 4D Analytical Tool (4-DAT). In: Proceedings of the European and Mediterranean Conference on Information Systems, pp. 1–8 (2006)
7. Rasool, G., Aftab, S., Hussain, S., Streitferdt, D.: eXRUP: a hybrid software development model for small to medium scale projects. J. Softw. Eng. Appl. **6**(9), 446 (2013)
8. Dalalah, A.: Extreme programming: strengths and weaknesses. Comput. Technol. Appl. **5**(1), 15–20 (2014)
9. Rao, K.N., Naidu, G.K., Chakka, P.: A study of the agile software development methods, applicability and implications in industry. Int. J. Softw. Eng. its Appl. **5**(2), 3545 (2011)
10. Ahmad, G., Soomro, T.R., Brohi, M.N.: XSR: novel hybrid software development model (Integrating XP, Scrum & RUP). Int. J. Soft Comput. Eng. (IJSCE) **2**(3), 126–130 (2014)

11. Anwer, F., Aftab, S., Shah, S.M., Waheed, U.: Comparative analysis of two popular agile process models: extreme programming and scrum. Int. J. Comput. Sci. Telecommun. **8**(2), 1–7 (2017)
12. Qureshi, M.R.J.: Agile software development methodology for medium and large projects. IET Softw. **6**(4), 358–363 (2012)
13. Aslam, N., Sarwar, N., Batool, A.: Designing a model for improving CPU scheduling by using machine learning. Int. J. Comput. Sci. Inf. Secur. **14**(10), 201 (2016)
14. Bilal, M., Sarwar, N., Saeed, M.S.: A hybrid test case model for medium scale web based applications. In: 2016 Sixth International Conference on Innovative Computing Technology (INTECH), pp. 632–637 (2016)
15. Bajwa, I.S., Sarwar, N.: Automated generation of express-g models using NLP. Sindh Univ. Res. J.-SURJ (Sci. Ser.) **48**(1), 5–12 (2016)
16. Cheema, S.M., Sarwar, N., Yousaf, F.: Contrastive analysis of bubble & merge sort proposing hybrid approach. In: 2016 Sixth International Conference on Innovative Computing Technology (INTECH), pp. 371–375 (2016)
17. Sarwar, N., Latif, M.S., Aslam, N., Batool, A.: Automated object role model generation. Int. J. Comput. Sci. Inf. Secur. **14**(9), 301–308 (2016)

Intelligent Systems

PACS: A Standardized Model
for the Deployment of Digital Imaging in DoR

Gulraiz Javaid Joyia[✉], Muhammad Talal, and Sunniya Ikram

Department of Software Engineering, The Islamia University of Bahawalpur, Bahawalpur,
Pakistan
ingrgulraiz@gmail.com

Abstract. In today's world Medical Record Systems (MRS) became a critical
parameter in making decisions, also an equivalent need for managing errors by
automated data practicing for quality assurance. There is no doubt that the Picture
Archiving and Communication System (PACS) is now a mature technology over
the past couple of years and is also implemented in many developed countries.
But still, the success of PACS is of major concern for the healthcare industry,
most importantly in developing countries like Pakistan. For this reason, it is the
primary purpose of our research that we introduce considerations for the design
and its solutions related to the practical implementation and evaluation of PACS
within the department of radiology (DoR) environment in Pakistan. Our research
also proposed the method for smooth transformation of the existing hospital environment to a digital Medical Record System (MRS) and the integration of PACS
within the hospital modalities using HL7 & DICOM medical standards, which
can also later be connected to other healthcare organizations.

Keywords: HL7 · PACS · MRS · Healthcare

1 Introduction

Advancement of technology in the domain of healthcare, specifically digital imaging,
and computation is developed to a level that now, it is possible to get the medical images
directly from modalities, save them on a computer, and later a doctor can view it for
diagnosis. A liquid crystal display (LCD) can be used to view the image at the place
of image capturing or at a distant location from that place. An image can be viewed
at different sites using multiple LCDs after a master copy of the image is saved, and
one copy will be transmitted to display the acquired image on the LCD [1]. MRS and
radiology information system (RIS) are the main parts of the Patient Record Keeping
System (PRKS). So, for the development of good PRKS; integration of both MRS and
RIS is very important.

Roberto Sanz-Requena et al. [2] discussed the importance of PACS, DICOM, and
CocoCloud. He introduced a cloud portal for Radiological Information System (RIS),
which allows doctors or technicians to access patient medical imaging data and their
medical reports. Roberto also highlighted some new software components, architecture

© Springer Nature Switzerland AG 2022
D. N. A. Jawawi et al. (Eds.): ESMoC 2021, CCIS 1615, pp. 55–63, 2022.
https://doi.org/10.1007/978-3-031-19968-4_6

design, validation methods, and requirements for the system. Patrícia Leite et al. [3] have discussed the vital role of Health Information Systems (HIS) and DICOM in the domain of medical imaging. Patricia tried to improve and evaluate DICOM by mentioning that her primary focus is to propose a methodology for DICOM functionality evaluation, a method for the questionnaire which will help characterize the level of functionality. Bing-jin Liang et al. [4] have introduced mobile base medical imaging using DICOM and Web Access to DICOM Objects (WADO); which is a web service. Bing also mention the testing of this on a different mobile platform like Andriod, IOS, and some other. The author mentioned the feature of the medical imaging tool for Andriod in his literature as well. M.S. Neofytou et al. [5] discussed how opensource software's in the domain of healthcare are a huge need of time and offer interoperability, flexibility, and resource-saving. Neofytou listed a few open-source service enablers among them author also listed and explained the importance of the PACS in medical imaging as a service enabler. Kenneth Heckman et al. [6] discusses the PACS architecture and how PACS is evolved? How today's PACS has integrated updated imaging techniques, computer systems utilization, and the use of networking technologies. Bakheet Aldosari et al. [7] has focused on the importance of acceptance of PACS, Bakheet believes that for any hospital it is vital to know the acceptance of PACS in the hospital environment rather than the importance of PACS deployment or integration. He did a strong survey on PACS at King Abdulaziz Medical City (KAMC), Riyadh, Saudi Arabia. In conclusion, he advised medical organizations to survey the acceptance of PACS to increase the productivity of the medical systems. Teresa C. Piliouras et al. [8] focus on the importance of digital information in the medical environment. Teresa discussed the challenges later faced after the implementation of new technology. Teresa also highlighted limitations of interoperability, and image sharing capabilities for the vendors of electronic health record (HER), and PACS. Alexandre Savaris et al. [9] have discussed the integration of PACS in the telemedicine system. Alexandre also mentioned both of these are separately located but combined to work as a whole. Alexandre is also aimed to standardize the procedures by adopting a standardized messaging framework. S. S. Cordeiro et al. [10] has presented checkpoints in the literature for the deployment of PACS and S. S. has also mapped these checkpoints to the risk table which was provided by European Union Agency for Network and Information Security (ENISA). Author also proposed and evaluated a risk model for PACS environment.

Figure 1 shows that 1) Is the internet, A) is PACS server, B) is a database server, C) is a web server, G) is a review station, H) is a reading station, E) is non-DICOM modalities, F) is gateways, and D) is DICOM modalities.

In the Department of Radiology (DoR), a patient faces a sequence of steps when he is first registered in the department till the time clinical diagnostic reports with the doctor's findings are issued. The point of interest is that the processes being followed is evolved, and this procedure will not be the optimum solution for DoR [11]. PACS installation will give a chance to evaluate and redesign an efficient workflow for DoR. Design consideration and its proposed solution related to the integration and implemen-network is required to retrieve and store data for good performance. tation of PACS within the environment of DoR in Pakistan was the aim of our research. The proposed research also presented a shift strategy to shift the hospital system smoothly to a digital one and also

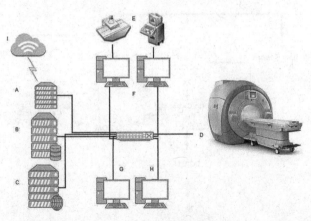

Fig. 1. Workflow of picture archiving and communication system shows a proper topological

the integration of all existing modalities to a centralized PACS which also can connect with other remote areas healthcare units and hospitals which lacks the primary medical facilities. The suggested deployment of the PACS and its analysis is also supported by an underlying case study in this paper to increase the system throughput of the system.

2 Methodology

PACS comprises data and image acquisition, storing, and displaying by the integration of networks and software applications. Its design focus is the connectivity of the system, the top-down and bottom-up engineering approach is implemented from a managerial point of view. In hospitals, PACS is an attractive tool for administration because it is a complete justification of return on investment (RoI) for analysis of the cost on it [12]. This system includes the features: standardization, expandability, open architecture and connectivity, reliability, robustness, fault tolerance, and cost-effectiveness.

In Fig. 2, it is shown how PACS is integrated with the MRS & a Modality using a middleware and also shows different medical standards used for standardized communication.

Well-known medical standards are very useful in the implementation of PACS. Notably Digital imaging and Communications in Medicine (DICOM) and Health Level 7–Fast Healthcare Interoperability Resources (HL7-FHIR). FHIR provides a framework for integration, exchange, retrieval, and sharing of information. It is also helpful in the domain of clinical practice, and re-evaluation of healthcare services. Hl7 standard is the highest-level standard, which works on the application layer of the Open Systems Interconnection (OSI) model [13]. On the other side, DICOM is a standard for storing, handling, transmitting, and printing medical images. It also deals with file formats and network protocols. For the communication between the systems, the TCP/IP protocol is used. DICOM standard files can be exchanged between two parties only if they are capable of receiving patient data and images in the DICOM format. It can also integrate different modalities of different manufactures into a PACS [14].

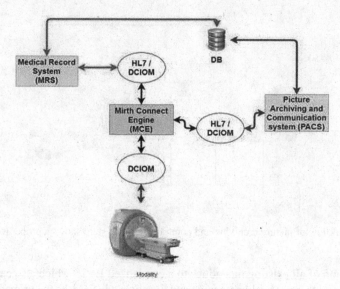

Fig. 2. Abstract level diagram

2.1 Healthcare Enterprise Integration

There is no doubt HL7 & DICOM are the best medical standards; which are compliant with the medical modalities and healthcare information systems. It is the basic requirement of the standardized medical systems to follow these medical standards; so, that the designed system will help to improvise the workflow of clinical operations. Integrating the Healthcare Enterprise (IHE) facilitates an information model and set of vocabulary; which is very helpful in using HL7 & DICOM standards for the DoR and transactions at the clinical level.

This set of vocabularies and models are also helpful on the user and technical team side for a better understanding of the smooth system integration. Below are some important factors for the integration of PACS:

Open Architecture and Connectivity. The Open Network Design (OND) was very important to use, as it allows the standardization technique for messaging and data exchange between the diverse systems. Computer communication systems change so rapidly that it is not a good choice to select a closed architecture which would be an obstacle to the system's upgradation.

System Reliability. In this healthcare enterprise environment, we considered PACS is a mission-critical system. So, it was important to measure fault tolerance, also logging, and error detection to improvise system reliability.

System Security. In the healthcare domain, the most confidential information is the patient data, for which the patient is more concerned. It is also important due to legal issues in the domain of healthcare. Our system proposed a sophisticated database system; which includes authorization and identification mechanisms by accounts, and passwords. Application software used to run PACS can provide further layers of protection.

2.2 Planning Process

During the process of planning; a survey was done in which bandwidth of the backbone and branches were accessed. In this regard guidelines on a minimum network, requirements were given by the PACS vendor. These requirements were also helpful during the survey.

Another important point is that the Radiology Information System (RIS) should meet the integration and installation requirements of PACS. Moreover, it is also important that how non-RIS images will be unified in the system. In this regard every piece of equipment should be recognized that it is DICOM compliant or not, it should not be done based on assumptions.

Further, a cost analysis for the equipment is required, which is to be upgraded for interoperability, as well as network point, desk, and power sockets, etc. The decisions about the existing data archives migration; both radiology examination requests and images were needed to be taken by local administrations. Here the term data migration means the data which is in the existing system and is needed to be transferred to the newly deployed system, which includes patient's demographics.

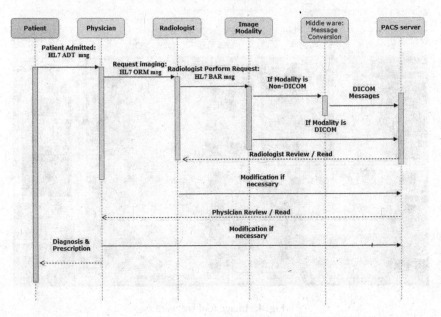

Fig. 3. Sequence diagram of flow of patient for PACS with HL7 & DICOM messages

In Fig. 3 sequence diagram is a clear depiction of how patient information will pass from the physicians, radiologists, towards and from PACS using HL7 and DICOM messages. It also shows a modality can be a DICOM or non-DICOM, in the case of Non-DICOM it will need a conversion of information to the DICOM standard. The DICOM & TCP/IP networking protocols are used for the communication purposes between MRS, middleware (message conversion), & DICOM modality. High-speed communication networks are used between the PACS controller and workstations for acquisition and sending large images to the PACS controller [15].

3 Deployment and Testing

To optimize the system performance, deployment and testing are very important. To do so, it was deployed in Rawalpindi. The complete system was basically of two parts MRS and PACS.

3.1 PACS

This software is used for the acquisition, storing, and reviewing of radiological acquired images. A DICOM web-enable viewer is used to display PACS in-home and clinical stations. It is also helpful in sending and getting online images from the PACS server and DICOM Modality.

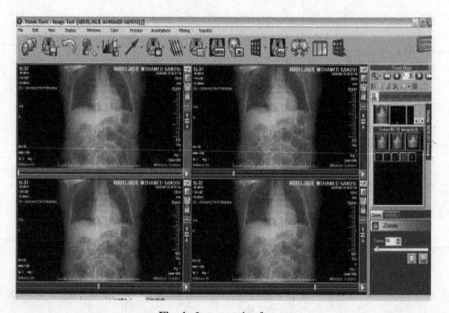

Fig. 4. Image tool software

In Table 1, the improvements after the installation of PACS are shown, overall, it was approximately 20% increase in the medical scans as compared to without PACS.

3.2 Testing of the System

After the design and development of the system, it is tested various times on prepared scenarios. Various inputs are given and outputs are confirmed what is expected. We have

Table 1. Improvement after installation of PACS

	Diagnostic X-Ray's	Mammography	CT Scan	Ultrasounds	Total
Before PACS attendees	143	74	61	95	373
After PACS attendees	172	87	78	112	449
	~ 20% increase	~ 18% increase	~ 28% increase	~ 18% increase	~ 20.5% increase

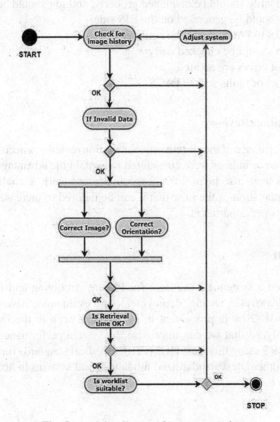

Fig. 5. Activity diagram for system testing

used fiber-optic connection with star topology between the PACS server, switch, web server, and archive server. For other devices, the T1 link is used in the network.

To evaluate the system performance and correctness exemplary test scripts were used as shown in Fig. 5. These test cases were used before the system installation and configuration and after the installation to remove if any error or tune the performance.

3.3 PACS Maintenance

Designing of working procedure was also necessary for the system, whose implementation may be unplanned or planned during the system downtime. Another important point is that the RIS and PACS databases should be synchronized and updated after resuming the system services. Following were the important points taken into consideration:

- Maintaining and checking the integrity of the database system $\surd$ Assuring that the correct image should be in the correct folder
- Order from RIS should be completed on PACS
- No order should be empty
- Worklist of modality should be displayed properly, nothing should be missed
- Correct codes should be generated on the RIS side
- Orders from RIS to PACS should be completed
- System backup should be checked daily
- RIS/PACS input errors are audited
- Correcting errors or faults sent to PACS

3.4 Implementation Review

To access the performance of the system implementation review is a necessary parameter. Different performance indices were considered to explain the advantages of the PACS. These parameters were also helpful for proposing future work & challenges. Table 1. Is also a clear explanation of the time that it can be tailored to increase the admittance number of patients per department.

4 Conclusion

We have discussed a systematic scenario for Picture Archiving and Communication System planning, analysis, testing, deployment, and evaluation. Also shown in Table 1 an overall approx. 20% improvement in radiological scan in the DoR. It was also observed and analyzed that we can improvise the system performance by integrating the PACS with MRS using the latest HL7 (FHIR) medical standards for integration and compliance with other latest standardized modalities and systems in healthcare.

References

1. Kormentzas, G., Maglogiannis, I., Vasis, D., Vergados, D., Rouskas, A.: A modeling and simulation framework for compound medical applications in regional healthcare networks. Int. J. Electron. Healthc. **1**, 427–441 (2005). April
2. Sanz-Requena, R., Mañas-García, A., Cabrera-Ayala, J.L., García-Martí, G.: A CloudBased Radiological Portal for the Patients: IT Contributing to Position the Patient as the Central Axis of the 21st Century Healthcare Cycles. In: 2015 IEEE/ACM 1st International Workshop on TEchnical and LEgal aspects of data pRivacy and SEcurity, pp. 54-57. Florence (2015). https://doi.org/10.1109/TELERISE.2015.18

3. Leite, P., Carvalho, S., Teixeira, P., Rocha, Á.: DICOM functionality assessment. In: 2017 12th Iberian Conference on Information Systems and Technologies (CISTI), pp. 1–4. Lisbon (2017). https://doi.org/10.23919/CISTI.2017.7975888

4. Liang, B., Lin, Y.: A web-based mobile medical image reading system. In: 2016 8th International Conference on Information Technology in Medicine and Education (ITME), pp. 50–53. Fuzhou (2016). https://doi.org/10.1109/ITME.2016.0021

5. Neofytou, M.S., et al.: Electronic health record application support service enablers. In: 2015 37th Annual International Conference of the IEEE Engineering in Medicine and Biology Society (EMBC), pp. 1401–1404. Milan (2015). https://doi.org/10.1109/EMBC.2015.731 8631

6. Heckman, K., Schultz, T.J.: PACS Architecture. In: Dreyer, K.J., Thrall, J.H., Hirschorn, D.S., Mehta, A. (eds.) PACS. Springer, New York, NY (2006). https://doi.org/10.1007/0-387-310 703_13

7. Aldosari, B.: User acceptance of a picture archiving and communication system (PACS) in a Saudi Arabian hospital radiology department. BMC Med Inform Decis Mak 12, 44 (2012). https://doi.org/10.1186/1472-6947-12-44

8. Piliouras, T.C., Suss, R.J., Yu, P.L.: Digital imaging & electronic health record systems: Implementation and regulatory challenges faced by healthcare providers. In: 2015 Long Island Systems, pp. 1-6. Applications and Technology, Farmingdale, NY (2015). https://doi.org/10. 1109/LISAT.2015.7160179

9. Savaris, A., Gimenes Marquez Filho, A.A., Rodrigues Pires de Mello, R., Colonetti, G.B., Von Wangenheim, A., Krechel, D.: Integrating a PACS network to a statewide telemedicine system: a case study of the santa catarina state integrated telemedicine and telehealth system. In: 2017 IEEE 30th International Symposium on Computer-Based Medical Systems (CBMS), pp. 356-357. Thessaloniki (2017). https://doi.org/10.1109/CBMS.2017.128

10. Cordeiro, S.D.S., SantAna, F.S., Suzuki, K.M.F., Azevedo-Marques, P.M.: A risk analysis model for PACS environments in the cloud. In: 2015 IEEE 28th International Symposium on Computer-Based Medical Systems, pp. 356-357. Sao Carlos (2015). https://doi.org/10.1109/ CBMS.2015.31

11. Paré, G., Aubry, D., Lepanto, L., Sicotte, C.: Evaluating PACS Success: a multidimensional model, hicss. In: Proceedings of the 38th Annual Hawaii International Conference on System Sciences (HICSS'05) - Track 6, p. 147c (2005)

12. Duncan, J.: Medical image analysis: progress over two decades and the challenges ahead. IEEE Trans. PAMI 22, 85–106 (2000). Jan.

13. Health Level Seven: Available at http://www.hl7.org/ Access date 23 November 2020

14. DICOM Standard 2003: Available at https://www.dicomstandard.org/ Access date 23 November 2020

15. Cashen, M.S., Dykes, P., Gerber, B.: eHealth technology and Internet resources: barriers for vulnerable populations. J. Cardiovas. Nurs. 19, 209–214 (2004 May/June)

Content-Based Venue Recommender Approach for Publication

Muhammad Umair[1]([✉]), Sohail Jabbar[2], Muhammad Arslan Rauf[1], Mujahid Rafiq[3], and Toqeer Mahmood[4]

[1] University of Electronic Science and Technology of China, Chengdu, China
muhammadumair894@gmail.com
[2] The University of Faisalabad, Faisalabad, Pakistan
[3] Zhengzhou University, Zhengzhou, China
[4] National Textile University, Faisalabad, Pakistan

Abstract. The recommendation system is used in every field where a user may observe several choices. A good recommendation may increase the user interest and lessen the resources concerning time and effort for selecting the most appropriate choice. Websites use cookies to know about users' preferences, likeness, and utilize user experiences to know about trending values. In this paper, a venue recommendation approach is proposed for research paper publications. The proposed recommendation technique utilizes a content-based approach using machine learning techniques to generate an appropriate recommendation. Feature engineering techniques including vector space, term frequency-inverse document frequency is used in this study. To classify the content, the Naïve Bayes probabilistic algorithm and support vector machine (SVM) is used. To achieve the objective, abstracts of the scientific publications published by Springer are extracted to make the dataset. The dataset consists of 100 different classes. The experimental results of the proposed technique exhibit more efficiency compared to the existing state-of-the-art technique by achieving more than 80% accuracy on the given dataset.

Keywords: Recommendation · Naïve Bayes · Support vector machine · Classification

1 Introduction

In the present era, people prefer recommendations to get an idea about something in which they are interested. The recommendation system is used everywhere to get appropriate suggestions in an environment where several choices are available. With the spread of extensive web-based information, almost all web-based services taking reviews from users to improve their web content. Famous search engines like YouTube and Google utilize user queries to improve their research results. Because of extensive corpora, it's a very difficult job for a website or a search engine to provide appropriate results to their user's demands.

© Springer Nature Switzerland AG 2022
D. N. A. Jawawi et al. (Eds.): ESMoC 2021, CCIS 1615, pp. 64–77, 2022.
https://doi.org/10.1007/978-3-031-19968-4_7

Nowadays recommendation systems are very popular in every field of life. Health care recommendation systems provide services to recommend medicines, movie websites use recommendation systems to suggest a movie to their visitor which is closer to their interest in watching.

Based on input data, there are three categories of recommender systems [1], collaborative filtering, content-based recommendation, and hybrid recommendation system. Collaborative filtering recommends by learning from the user's previous rating or browsing history of the user. The content-based recommendation used the description of the product and the user's profile to generate the recommended items. Content-based recommendation methods use preference information and behavior information generated by the user in the past without using the personal information and item description information, preference, and the user's rating about an item. The hybrid recommendation combines both characteristics of content-based and collaborative based recommendation. Because of content-based recommendation algorithms, privacy issues emerge as the most internet user public their personal data online. The collaborative based recommendation also has some drawback like very sparse users rating may affect recommendation results.

The collaborative-based recommendation also suffers problems like if an item having not past feedback, then the item couldn't show to the user as a recommendation, so we can only use a collaborative approach when we already have users' feedback. The feedback of an item can be obtained in different ways like some time you have to credit some rating number to an item or you choose a rating star. These types of ratings are used in online e-commerce sites and for audio, video content available online [2]. The recommendation results purely dependent on user scores are given to a particular item. Some other type of applications of recommendation systems demands a different type of feedback like if you want to suggest a book to a reader, you know books read by the user, which type of content he/she likes, and so you can suggest a new one to them. These types of recommendations are required to extract term frequency from the content and then by applying some weights on them by using some clustering algorithms so that these vectors can be classified.

Text classification [3] is a fundamental development in trademark tongue handling. It might be performed using unique classification algorithms. In Machine Learning, the classifier is fabricated consequently by taking in the properties of classifications from a lot of pre-characterized training data. Naive Bayes and support vector machines are popular machine learning algorithms. We use both algorithms in our study for the sake of classifying textual data. For this study, abstracts of journals from springer extracted through a specially designed web crawler. The results of this study show a significant improvement in recommendations concerning previously state-of-the-art techniques. Naïve Bayes achieves more than 80% accuracy on the available dataset. Text classification is a significant and normal errand in administered artificial intelligence. Its application is email spam recognition, assessment investigation, language discovery of composed content, characterization, and so on. Numerous classifiers can be utilized for record characterization. Some of them are neural systems, bolster vector machines, hereditary calculations, Naive Bayes classifier, k-nearest neighbors, and Rocchio classifier.

The paper is divided into five major sections. In Sect. 1, A brief introduction to the work is presented. In Sect. 2, the literature review is present. In Sect. 3, the research methodology of the presented work is discussed. The experimental results are depicted in Sect. 4 and Sect. 5 consists of the conclusion.

2 Related Work

At the starting of the 20th century, a lot of work has done in the field of recommendation. A trust network named TidalTrust for prediction proposed by Golbeck extends the breadth-first search method. This system finds raters with the minimum path distance by the user and aggregates their opinion to the trust rating between the weighted values [4]. Luong et al. [5] recommend the publication venue to the researchers by exploring their network history. For this recommender system, the ACM data set was used. New researchers have difficulty submitting their papers after completing the work. To resolve this problem, Zaihan Yang et al. [6] provide a venue recommendation model to all the new scientists. This collaborative filtering-based recommender system used real-world data set of ACM and Cite Seer libraries. Abdulrhman et al. [7] proposed a venue-based recommendation system to publish a research article. They provide a similarity learning technique by using metadata and related cited papers.

The confidence score was measured by similarity citation network metrics. Margaris et al. [8] propose a venue recommender approach for social network users by considering rating prediction, venue QoS, similarity, and distance metrics. Xi Wang et al. [9] make a comparison of user rating and sentiment analysis to judge the performance of the venue recommendation system. A neural network-based sentiment analyzer was used to measure the effectiveness by replacing user ratings with sentiment information like or dislike words. Makbule Gulcin Ozsoy proposes a new method named "FastText" for venue recommendation [10]. Iyer et al. [11] provide a recommendation system that recommends the best conference for the authors where acceptance chances would be higher. The authors used correspondence analysis with dimensionality reduction and topic modeling methods. Patra et al. [12] propose a content-based recommender system for literature work recommendation based on similar data set. Dehdarirad et al. [13] provide a systematic literature review on scholarly publication venue recommendations.

Text Classification is significant in the vast majority of the information recovery frameworks. Ranjitha et al. [14] propose an artificial intelligence way to deal with process and order content information. Naive Bayes is utilized as a classifier to anticipate what information is valuable in thinking about the text. They add data and divide into two parts, In the first training they see the probability of class and its feature and in the second phase, they compute the maximum value and features given to the class. The Classifier could have a place with Gaussian Naïve Bayes, Bernoulli Guileless Bayes, or Multinomial Naïve Bayes. The exhibition assessment results for characterization procedure are thought about with Hadoop Map Reduce to that with Naive Bayes classifiers utilizing Naive Bayes strategy is much better and effectively used when contrasted with the order system utilizing K-Nearest Neighbor in Hadoop structure. Donghui Wang et al. [15] proposed a content-based conference and journal recommender system. The authors used chi-square feature selection by using term frequency, inverse document term frequency, and SoftMax regression to predict suitable venues for submitting a publication.

Haifeng Liu et al. [16] provide citation recommender systems by applying context-based collaborative filtering methods. CCF method recommends papers of the same target for citation. They measure the similarity between cited papers by the pair-wise collection of contexts.

Zun Hlaing Moe et al. [17] compare the classification algorithms to measure the more accurate classifier. For this purpose, the authors classify documents into ten categories of IT field papers. The result shows that the Support vector machine is more accurate than the Naïve Bayes classifier. Han Liu et al. [18] propose a modified fuzzy technique for hate speech classification. The authors used four types of speeches including race, religion, sex, and disability. Performance is measured by comparing it with the previous fuzzy approach.

Shaohua Gao et al. [19] proposed a semantical similarity approach to recommend items for geosciences. For this purpose, Metadata of geosciences attributes was used. Lei Xu et al. [20] introduce a semantical relatedness approach for the reduction of the dimensionality of the microblog. Semantic analysis improves the recommendation of a deep learning approach. Wang Zhou et al. [21] use latent interests for each user, capture factors contextual information via a convolutional neural network, and review them. For more improvement, DLMR uses the ranking of the candidate's through three layers and denoising auto-encoder from heterogeneous information. Toan et al. [22] proposed a group recommendation system for the common interest of a group. Group recommendation is a difficult job because many peoples in a group may have a different preference for an item, maximal verity of information, and maximal group utility algorithm used in real-world data to extract a versatile group recommendation. Shehata et al. [23] proposed a concept-based mining system for text documentation. In statistical analysis, they use the term either to use a phrase or word. This approach finds how important a term in a document using term frequency. The proposed system is capable to extract important terms concerning their semantic used in the document and discriminate non-important terms. The given model also shows a significant improvement in the clustering of text documentation. Kowsari et al. [24] proposed a text classification technique by combining deep learning methods. The proposed scheme is named as deep learning-based hierarchically text classifier. Buzic et al. [25] predict the song performer by using a naïve bayes classifier based on lyrics.

Traditional approaches use natural language processing and statistical methods which use the frequency of a term to consider it's a quality phrase. To overcome this difficulty, Bing Li et al. [26] proposed an automated quality phrase mining approach to mine quality phrases from massive text corpora. Zhiquan Wang et al. [27] proposed a support vector machine (SVM) and convolutional neural network (CNN) based approach to classifying web-based text. The proposed approach consists of five layers, which extract text features from the web and SVM provides the classification and prediction of that text. An et al. [28] proposed an algorithm for testing the performance and texting of the songs. The formula is based on class, documentation, class possibility, the possibility of the documentation, and the algorithm is classified by computational competence, low modification, incremental learning, direct forecast of following likelihood, strength on the missing value of noise.

3   Research Methodology

This study is based on a novel technique that is used as a recommendation system to extract the most suitable journal. The recommendation system uses Bayes probabilistic classification with a frequency-based feature method for the recommendation of most appropriate journals to the authors. This study presented a content-based recommendation approach for computer science journals concerning their similarity level to submit research work. This study used a web crawler, with the help of it we got a dataset from the springer web. Naïve Bayes probabilistic classification model and support vector machine used as classifiers. The system recommends the top best and most relevant journal to users by taking input abstract of the paper.

Here is a list of steps of how our study proceeds:

3.1   Data Collection

For this study, we manage to have a dataset of 10,000 abstracts. These abstracts belong to 100 different journals. For the sake of equal opportunity, we set a file with 100 abstracts, which means that we have 100 files and every file has 100 abstracts. In data files, there are two columns, the first column having abstract text and the second column having the name of the journal from which abstract belongs. These dataset files belong to Springer, which is an American based online Publishing Company. Thanks to them for allowing us to get this dataset while other publication companies had a restriction on their web resources. For this sake, we form a web scraper in python.

3.2   Data Preprocessing

Preprocessing (Fig. 1) is the first step to increase the performance and efficiency of the classified documents. This process involves the clearing of the text document from unwanted information. This categorized as punctuation marks, stop words, numeric, symbols, and case conversion. This text data belongs to multiple language standards, like ASCII, UNI code, UTF, etc. So, we need to set this out, we use the UTF-8 encoding scheme in all our text processing. It's a variable-length encoding scheme that incorporates both ASCII and Unicode standards text. As we explained earlier, our dataset contains 100 files of text abstracts. For storing and computational purposes, we use the ".CSV" file format for this study because it's easy to do some computational work in the ".CSV" format. Our CSV file has two columns, the first column having the name "Text" which means it contains the abstract, and the second column named" Label" which is the class or name of the journal from which the abstracts belong. As we now text documents contain much more irrelevant information which has nothing to do with computation. We need to get rid of them so that we have a clean dataset that will be used for further computational tasks. So, for data preprocessing we split preprocessing into multiple steps.

Tokenization. The first step in our study to preprocess our dataset. The token can be defined as each "entity" that is part of what is divided, based on principles. For example, each word is a symbol when the word has the phrase "symbol". If you have separated phrases in a paragraph, each sentence can also become a token. For this purpose, we use an NLP library named "Natural Language Toolkit" and use its tokenized function. Here is an example of it.

Text = "this is a sample text for tokenization process explanation".
Here is the text we got after applying tokenization.
['this', 'is', 'a', 'sample', 'text', 'for', 'tokenization', 'process', 'explanation',]
We see tokenization forms an array of tokens.

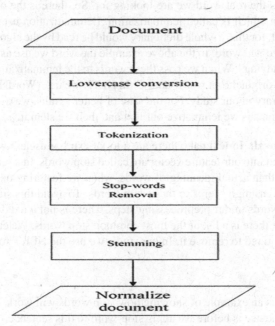

Fig. 1. Data preprocessing flow chart

Stemming and Lemmatization. The idea of stemming is a kind of standardization method. Many variations of words have the same meaning, except when time is involved.

The reason we base ourselves is to shorten the search and normalize the sentences. Let's consider an example,

"I am drinking water" can be converted to" I drink water"

In the above sentences, both mean the same thing. I was the same. The sentence clearly shows the meaning of drinking water in both sentences,

How many times affixes we put on a word to use it in our sentences. So, to deal with this type of issue we use stemmer to cut these affixes from the word and keep its root values. There are many stemmers available but, in our study, we use the "Poster stemmer" algorithm which was developed in 1979. We used porter-stemmer from the NLTK.

Text = ['work', 'works', 'worked', 'working'].

The output we got after giving the above sample text to poster-stemmer is [Work, Work, Work, Work].

A lit bit problem will occur with a stemmer when we have words like study, studies, and studying. The stemmer algorithm will cutoff suffixes and cause misleading.

For example, if the stemmer goes through words "studying" & "Studies", it will cut off "ing" from the first word and cut "ies" from the second word, after stemming process the word we left with is "study" and "stud" simultaneously. We can observe that the word "stud" is the root word we are looking for. So, there is the other concept for text normalization which is called lemmatization. Lemmatization uses morphological analysis of the text, for this, a whole dictionary would be read by the algorithm and match every word to its rooted word. In the above example the word we use as sample text like "studies" and "studying". When we pass these words to the lemmatization algorithm the output will be the original root word "study". In NLTK we use "WordNet-Lemmatizer" from the stem library in our study. For the sake of better results, we use lemmatization before stemming means we lemmatize our text and then we stem it.

Stop Word Removal: In-text data, there are a lot of extra or useless words which will not be incorporated into our feature vector are called stop words. In a sentence, there are more stop words than actual meaningful words, when we featuring our feature vector, the algorithm assigns high scores to these stop words. To avoid this situation, we need to remove these words in our preprocessing steps. There is not a fixed or universal list for stop words but there is a list of the most common stop words. We can add manually as much as we required to remove it. In our study, we use the NLKT for removing stop words too.

For example
Text = "This is an example of showing how stop words will work".
The above sentence is before we apply stop-word to this sentence.
Output after applying the stop-word algorithm to this sentence.
['This', 'example', 'showing', 'stop', 'words', 'work',]
We can see from the example that the words like "is", "an", "of", "how", "will" are removed from the text. So, we have actual features of the text which will help us to get some knowledge about the sentences.

3.3 Feature Engineering

Features are the metrics in which the fate of a document can be decided, in simple words these are the key points about which we can decide the nature of some text. Every word in text behaves like a feature. In-text preprocessing step we remove stop words and punctuation and other irrelevant stuff from the text to get these things out from our decision-making process. There are many ways to construct a feature vector. A feature vector (Fig. 2) state that a list or array which contains the number of words belongs to text after preprocessing. Particularly when we talk about text data, there is a bit of confusion about how to get the right features from the massive text. There is no standard definition of a good or bad feature, but there are many techniques to get the right features from the text. Here, we discuss some of them which are used in this paper. Before getting into the depth of this we should talk about the qualities of a good feature vector. A good feature vector should not overfit the model. Mean as fewer duplicate data we have, there is less chance of overfitting. The second thing is that your data must not mislead your model because it will affect your decision which the model learns from misleading feature data. There should be clean and normalized data before considering it for the feature.

The third and computationally important thing is don't try to make a very lengthy feature vector just to think that as much data we have in the feature set the more it easy to make a decision. The more the feature vector contains data the more it takes computationally power to process and may affect the performance of the system. So, for the sake of performance, the feature vector should be as small as possible covering all aspects of the text. That is why the selection of a good feature vector is very important because a system may change its outcomes if there not a good feature engineering method behind it.

Here are a few feature vectors techniques that we incorporate in our study.

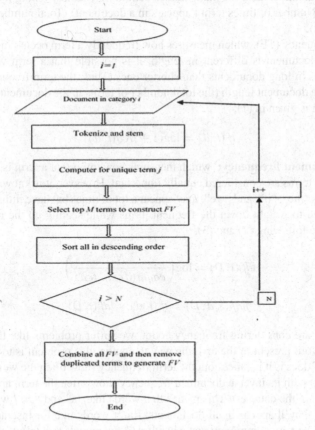

Fig. 2. Feature engineering flow chart

Count Vector: count vectors are referring to counting each word present in the text and assign a unique identification to it. When we are dealing with the massive dataset, there are frequent words present in the text but they're not having such significance but this algorithm doesn't notice this and treats every word equally. Count-Vectorizer gives you a vector that indicates how many times each word appears in the document. This is especially problematic because commonly used words such as "a", "the", "and", "a" etc. occur most of the time and other words contain the subject matter of your document will be less common. For example, if you're training a classifier to identify documents that relate to AI, you do not want them to learn words like "one" and "that," as they are unbound in every document (in terms of AI). Also, the number of occurrences of these non-thematic terms is significantly higher than in all other terms. This forces them to have the highest weight in the model because of their high incidence and distorts their model.

Term frequency-inverse document frequency is another way of setting up feature vectors. We can understand the mathematics behind it by simply listing it down as,

TF(t) = (Number of times term t appears in a document) (Total number of terms in the document).

Term frequency (TF), which measures how frequently a term occurs in a document. Since every document is different in length, it is possible that a term would appear frequent times in long documents than shorter ones. Thus, the term frequency is often divided by the document length (the total number of terms in the document) as a way of normalization is given in (1),

$$tf(t, d) = \log(1 + freq(t, d)) \tag{1}$$

Inverse Document Frequency: which measures how important a term is. While computing TF, all terms are considered equally important. However, it is known that certain terms, such as "the", "it", and "we", may appear a lot of times but have little importance. Thus, we need to weight down the frequent terms while scaling up the rare ones, by computing the following (2) and (3),

$$idf(t, D) = \log\left(\frac{N}{count(d \in D : t \in d)}\right) \tag{2}$$

$$tfidf(t, d, D) = tf(t, d) \times idf(t, D) \tag{3}$$

When we are considering frequency count, we suffer problems like the algorithm count every word present in the text, the way to combat this problem is to use TF-IDF. What TF-IDF does is it balances out the term frequency (how often the word appears in the document) with its inverse document frequency (how often the term appears across all documents in the data set). This means that words like "a" and "the" will have very low scores as they'll appear in all documents. Rarer words like for instance "machine learning" will be very common in just a handful of documents that talk about computer science or AI. TF-IDF will give higher scores to these words and thus they'll be the ones that the model identifies as important and tries to learn.

At the word-level, we construct a matrix that represents term frequency-inverse document frequency scores of every term in different documents. We use the scikit-learn package for these operations. Scikit-learn is a free machine learning library for multiple operations like classification, regression, and having built-in algorithms for these purposes.

N-grams are the combination of N terms together. This means several n items combine and we count them as a feature vector. More the number of n the bigger the feature vector is. For example, we have a text like "the is a sample text" and we want to apply n-gram and the n is two, in this case, the feature vector will consider adjacent words as a feature. For the above, we have a feature like [this is', 'is a', 'a sample', 'sample text'. So, we can understand how the n-gram works. The Matrix represents the TF-IDF scores of N-grams which are defined in the code.

Character level term frequency means we are splitting our words into characters. The same method for the previous two techniques was implemented here. These are the variation of feature vectors for text data as we see we can count a whole word or combine n-words or we can count only one character as a feature. In this study, we use all of them to see how they affect our results.

3.4 Classification

After the feature vector, the main task is to classify our text into classes in which they belong. We have 100 classes with each one has 100 abstracts. We trained our text to a machine learning model and after training out, the model would classify unseen text to the class the text belongs to. Many classifiers are there like liner classifier, Naïve Bayes, support vector machine, decision tresses, and neural networks. This study considered Naïve Bayes, a probabilistic model, and a support vector machine in our study. The performance of the system directly depends on how the system learns and then classifies the unseen data so there should be a good classifier so that we can accurately classify our dataset.

Naïve Bayes is a probabilistic model. It classifies based on maximum likelihood. Naïve Bayes model learns the features from the feature vector and when we exposed our model to unseen data, they can check maximum likelihood from learning data and set a suitable class to unseen data. We have 100 different classes so; we have used the variation of the Naïve Bayes model called Multinomial Naive Bayes.

Multinomial Naïve Bayes is a multiclass probabilistic model which suits our requirement. We can discuss some mathematical notation of the multinomial model.

Given a feature vector $X = (x_1, x_2, ..., x_n)$ and a class variable C_i, Bayes Theorem states that:

$$Prob\frac{C_i}{X} = \frac{Prob\ (X|C_i)P(C_i)}{Prob(X)}, for\ i = 1, 2, 3, ... I \qquad (4)$$

where $P(C_i|X)$ the posterior probability, $P(X|C_i)$ the likelihood, $P(C_i)$ the prior probability of a class, and $P(X)$ the prior probability of predictor. We are interested in calculating the posterior probability from the likelihood and prior probabilities. in our study, we split our data into a training set and test set, we train naïve bayes on multiple training sets like 90%, 80%, and 60% of the data. For testing purposes, we again test our algorithm on the multiple test samples. For final accuracy scores, we took the mean average of our results.

Support vector machine is also a supervised learning algorithm, based on a given dataset and features, it can able to draw a line between different data classes.

The proposed method is to select features concerning a selection metric. The feature engineering process removes duplicate text from feature vector and selects a high informative feature from the metric and Bayes classifier to classify data set to the multiclass category for an appropriate selection of a particular class of journals. We use feature vectors (Count Vectors, TF-IDF Vectors, Word level, N-Gram level) which we discussed earlier.

4 Results

The results of our study are listed below in Table 1, we can conclude that the Naïve Bayes classification approach with four different feature engineering techniques gives us nearly similar results. We use accuracy, precision, recall, and f-measure score to validate our results. We select four different feature selection because we need to test the accuracy of every feature, all the techniques choose the best features from the list, count vector technique just count the number of the word in the text document and forms a vector, similarly word-level term frequency-inverse document frequency select words but it measures the importance of a word or feature in the document. So, when there are duplicate features, this technique performs better to lesson down the weight of frequent words most of the time they are not important ones in the document. Word level TF-IDF performs well in cases where words are the most prominent features for a class to be recognized. Most of the time in sentiment analysis, the words feature plays the important task of assigning polarity score to the word but in our case, we are looking for the words which will describe the class of a document so that our algorithm will easily suggest the desired class when algorithm faces an unseen data. The feature vector formed by n-gram level term frequency is another variation in which n number of words combine to form a feature. This type of feature vector support classification when terms are important in classification. Character level TF-IDF will get characters in the text and form a feature vector of it. It seems to be less important but the results show that this feature vector comes up with a very good accuracy score.

Table 1. Results after applying Naïve Bayes with different feature vector technique

Models Metrics	Count Vector	Word level TF-IDF	N-gram level TF-IDF	Character level TF-IDF
Accuracy %	82.59	86.12	94.21	92.45
F-measure	0.78	0.82	0.92	0.90
Recall	0.82	0.86	0.94	0.93
Precision	0.77	0.79	0.91	0.88

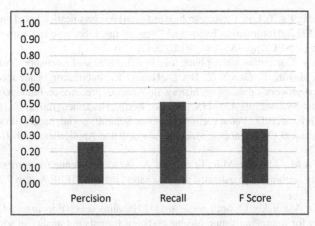

Fig. 3. Accuracy score with support vector machine

Figure 3 shows the results of the support vector machine algorithm using the n-gram feature engineering technique. The results show a very low score of accuracy measures. So, we clearly say that the SVM does not gain much accuracy regarding text multiclass classification. The accuracy score of SVM is 50%, with comparison to Naïve Bayes it's a low score. Naïve Bayes no doubt the best classifier concerning SVM. Support Vector perfume well in case of binary classification, in our study, we are classifying 100 classes. So, the algorithm behaves like one verse all that is why the accuracy measures and f score show the results not much appreciated.

5   Conclusion

Recommendations improve our decision-making process. This study presents a recommendation approach toward publication recommendation. This study shows an average of 89% accuracy, we use four feature engineering techniques in this study. Four multiple types of techniques are then classified by the Naïve Bayes algorithm to check their probabilistic score towards recommendations. We found that n-gram feature vector techniques perform better among the other three techniques that we used in our study. We use the SVM algorithm with n-gram feature engineering techniques to classify our dataset. SVM shows fewer accuracy towards this problem. F score supports the accuracy of our study with 0.86 on the average in the case of Naïve Bayes.

References

1. Ricci, F., Rokach, L., Shapira, B.: Recommender systems: introduction and challenges. In: Recommender systems handbook, pp. 1–34. Springer, Boston, MA (2015)
2. Yadav, R., Choorasiya, A., Singh, U., Khare, P., Pahade, P.: A Recommendation System for E-Commerce Base on Client Profile. In: 2018 2nd International Conference on Trends in Electronics and Informatics (ICOEI), pp. 1316–1322. IEEE (2018)

3. Liu, P., Yu, H., Xu, T., Lan, C.: Research on archives text classification based on Naive Bayes. In: 2017 IEEE 2nd Information Technology, Networking, Electronic and Automation Control Conference (ITNEC), pp. 187–190. IEEE (2017)
4. Golbeck, J.A.: Computing and applying trust in web-based social networks. PhD diss. (2005)
5. Luong, H., Huynh, T., Gauch, S., Do, L., Hoang, K.: Publication venue recommendation using author network's publication history. In: Asian Conference on Intelligent Information and Database Systems, pp. 426–435. Springer, Berlin, Heidelberg (2012)
6. Yang, Z., Davison, B.D.: Venue recommendation: Submitting your paper with style. In: 2012 11th International Conference on Machine Learning and Applications, vol. 1, pp. 681–686. IEEE (2012)
7. Alshareef, A.M., Alhamid, M.F., El Saddik, A.: Academic venue recommendations based on similarity learning of an extended nearby citation network. IEEE Access 7, 38813–38825 (2019)
8. Margaris, D., Vassilakis, C., Spiliotopoulos, D.: Handling uncertainty in social media textual information for improving venue recommendation formulation quality in social networks. Soc. Netw. Anal. Min. 9(1), 1–19 (2019). https://doi.org/10.1007/s13278-019-0610-x
9. Wang, X., Ounis, I., Macdonald, C.: Comparison of sentiment analysis and user ratings in venue recommendation. In: European Conference on Information Retrieval, pp. 215–228. Springer, Cham (2019)
10. Ozsoy, M.G.: Utilizing FastText for Venue Recommendation. arXiv preprint arXiv: 2005. 12982 (2020)
11. Iyer, R.R., Sharma, M., Saradhi, V.: A correspondence analysis framework for author-conference recommendations. arXiv preprint arXiv: 2001.02669 (2020)
12. Patra, B.G., Maroufy, V., Soltanalizadeh, B., Deng, N., Zheng, W.J., Roberts, K., Wu, H.: A content-based literature recommendation system for datasets to improve data reusability-a case study on gene expression omnibus (GEO) datasets. Journal of Biomedical Informatics, 103399 (2020)
13. Dehdarirad, H., Ghazimirsaeid, J., Jalalimanesh, A.: Scholarly publication venue recommender systems. Data Technologies and Applications (2020)
14. Ranjitha, K.V., Venkatesh Prasad, B.S.: Optimization Scheme for Text Classification Using Machine Learning Naïve Bayes Classifier. In: ICDSMLA 2019, pp. 576–586. Springer, Singapore (2020)
15. Wang, D., Liang, Y., Dong, X., Feng, X., Guan, R.: A content-based recommender system for computer science publications. Knowl.-Based Syst. 157, 1–9 (2018)
16. Liu, H., Kong, X., Bai, X., Wang, W., Megersa Bekele, T., Xia, F.: Context-based collaborative filtering for citation recommendation. IEEE Access 3, 1695–1703 (2015)
17. Moe, Z.H., San, T., Khin, M.M., Tin, H.M.: Comparison of Naive Bayes and support vector machine classifiers on document classification. In: 2018 IEEE 7th Global Conference on Consumer Electronics (GCCE), pp. 466–467. IEEE (2018)
18. Liu, H., Burnap, P., Alorainy, W., Williams, M.L.: A fuzzy approach to text classification with two-stage training for ambiguous instances. IEEE Transactions on Computational Social Systems 6(2), 227–240 (2019)
19. Gao, S., Song, J., Zhu, Y., Ma, C.: Association and recommendation for geosciences data attribute based on semantic similarity measurement. In: 2018 7th International Conference on Agro-geoinformatics (Agro-geoinformatics), pp. 1–5. IEEE (2018)
20. Xu, L., Jiang, C., Ren, Y.: Deep learning in exploring semantic relatedness for microblog dimensionality reduction. In: 2015 IEEE Global Conference on Signal and Information Processing (GlobalSIP), pp. 98–102. IEEE (2015)
21. Zhou, W., Li, J., Zhang, M., Wang, Y., Shah, F.: Deep learning modeling for top-n recommendation with interests exploring. IEEE Access 6, 51440–51455 (2018)

22. Toan, N.T., Cong, P.T., Tam, N.T., Viet Hung, N.Q., Stantic, B.: Diversifying group recommendation. IEEE Access **6**, 17776–17786 (2018)
23. Shehata, S., Karray, F., Kamel, M.: An efficient concept-based mining model for enhancing text clustering. IEEE Trans. Knowl. Data Eng. **22**(10), 1360–1371 (2009)
24. Kowsari, K., Brown, D.E., Heidarysafa, M., Meimandi, K.J., Gerber, M.S., Barnes, L.E.: Hdltex: Hierarchical deep learning for text classification. In: 2017 16th IEEE international conference on machine learning and applications (ICMLA), pp. 364–371. IEEE (2017)
25. Bužić, D., Dobša, J.: Lyrics classification using naive bayes. In: 2018 41st International Convention on Information and Communication Technology, Electronics and Microelectronics (MIPRO), pp. 1011–1015. IEEE (2018)
26. Li, B., Yang, X., Wang, B., Cui, W.: Efficiently Mining High Quality Phrases from Texts. In: AAAI, pp. 3474–3481 (2017)
27. Wang, Z., Qu, Z.: Research on Web text classification algorithm based on improved CNN and SVM. In: 2017 IEEE 17th International Conference on Communication Technology (ICCT), pp. 1958–1961. IEEE (2017)
28. An, Y., Sun, S., Wang, S.: Naive Bayes classifiers for music emotion classification based on lyrics. In: 2017 IEEE/ACIS 16th International Conference on Computer and Information Science (ICIS), pp. 635–638. IEEE (2017)

Determining Object Color in Images Using Color Thresh-Holding Approach

Marina Rasheed$^{(\boxtimes)}$ (iD)

Department of Computer Science, University of Sargodha, Sargodha, Pakistan
`mareena.rasheed@iub.edu.pk`

Abstract. In this article, we proposed a singular technique to hit upon the user-decided on color from an RGB photo the usage of color thresh-conserving technique. Our proposed technique use the color variations of low- and excessive-color pixel values and the usage of this distinction we expand a color masks photo. This ensuing color masks photo is then implemented at the authentic photo and executed bitwise AND operation to hit upon the photo vicinity having identical color location as of the distinction of the excessive and occasional stage pixel values. All this method is began out from changing the RGB to grey scale photo and the usage of median clear out to compress the noisy data. The proposed technique is applied in Python surroundings giving promising results. The proposed technique is similarly relevant in some of photo processing packages namely, the robots utilized in spy-associated activities, multi-item tracking, separation of the gadgets from the photo historical past primarily based totally at the color information, intrusion detection etc.

Keywords: RGB image · Color detection · Color thresh-holding · Image filtering

1 Introduction

The color intensity is considered as one of the fundamental and most important characteristics of an RGB image. If the color in a live video streaming or some digital image is detected successfully, the results can be used in a number of industrial and scientific applications [1–3]. The process of color detection involves a series of sub processes like image conversion, segmentation, filtering etc.

An image can be represented in a number of color models like gray-scale, Red Green Blue (RGB); hue, saturation, lightness (HSV) etc. In the conventional RGB model, the color of the image is detected [4, 5]. Furthermore, it also assists in adding these colors a number of ways to generate a wide range of colors. In RGB model, an image has the composition of 3-D matrix of $m \times n \times 3$ pixels with m rows and n columns of pixels for each red, green and blue color components of an image.

D. N. A. Jawawi et al. (Eds.): ESMoC 2021, CCIS 1615, pp. 78–83, 2022.
https://doi.org/10.1007/978-3-031-19968-4_8

2 Methodology

It is of key importance that how an image is perceived by the computer system since the image consists of a lot of pixels where each pixel corresponds to a unique code. The entire image is composed by the summation of these codes. These codes are then analyzed to define the color saturation and labeling of the color codes. In Fig. 1, we have presented the framework of our proposed approach.

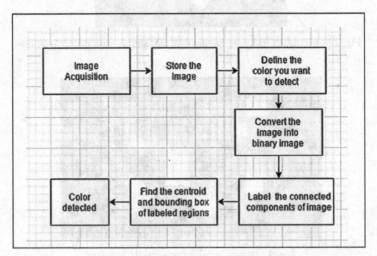

Fig. 1. Flowchart of proposed approach

3 Implementation

The first step in this process is to convert the RGB image to gray level and then binary in order to examine the in depth properties of the image. After detecting the edges and shape boundaries, the RGB color space is converted to L*a*b color scheme [6–8]. The novelty of our approach lies in the fact that we used the new color scheme mentioned above since this approach expresses the pixel color value in three different dimensions: $L*$ for the brightness feature ranging from black (0) to white (100), a* ranging from green (−) to red (+), and b* represents blue (−) to yellow (+). The L*a*b* conspire was created such that similar measure of mathematical change in these qualities ought to be generally projected to a similar measure of outwardly seen change.

The Fig. 2 represents the RGB image that will be analyzed for color detection of different shapes.

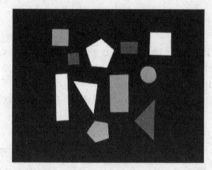

Fig. 2. Original RGB image having different shapes with different colors

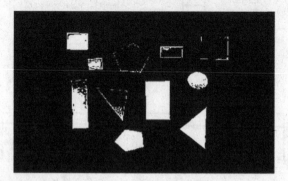

Fig. 3. Binary image of original RGB image

Similarly, Fig. 3 shows the binary form of the original image. In order to actually label and apply tag to the regions of an image capable enough to perceive a certain amount of color information; we compute the Euclidean distance among the dataset of known colors and the means of a particular image region. To identify the color, the minimum Euclidean distance among the data points will be chosen for the color identification.

In the primary step, we set the foreground place of the masks to white and the background of the photo to black. We will carry out the essential computations inside the masked (white) place of the photo and attempt to erode the masked barely to make certain facts are handiest being computed for the masked place and that no historical past is by accident included (because of a non-best segmentation of the form from the unique photo, for instance).

3.1 Lab Color Scheme

Back in 1976, the International Commission on Illumination (abridged CIE) fostered the CIE L*a*b* or here and there casually shortened as "Lab"). As referenced before, the picture tone is communicated in three qualities: L* for the delicacy from dark (0) to white (100), a* from green (−) to red (+), and b* from blue (−) to yellow (+). Besides, the CIELAB was intended for accomplishing the reason for utilizing similar measure of mathematical change in these qualities compares to generally a similar measure of outwardly seen change.

The critical component in curiosity of this plan lies in the truth this is gadget fair and does now never again care of characterizing the tones freely of the manner in which they're made or shown. The CIELAB shading region is ordinarily utilized while pix for print should be changed from RGB to CMYK, on the grounds that the CIELAB range comprises of each the arrays of the RGB and CMYK shading models.

Practically speaking, the distance is normally deliberate onto a third-dimensional range area for superior portrayal, and on this manner the L*, a*, and b* values are generally outright, with a pre-characterized range. The delicacy esteem, L*, addresses the haziest darkish at L* = zero, and the maximum excellent white at L* = one hundred. The shading channels, a* and b*, cope with real nonpartisan dim characteristics at a* = zero and b* = zero. The a* hub addresses the inexperienced–crimson part, with inexperienced the bad manner and crimson the wonderful manner. The b* hub addresses the blue–yellow part, with blue the bad manner and yellow the wonderful manner. The scaling and cutoff factors of the a* and b* tomahawks will rely on the specific execution, as depicted beneath, but they regularly run with inside the scope of ±one hundred or −128 to +127 (marked 8-digit range).

The CIELAB shading region became gotten from the past "ace" CIE 1931 XYZ shading region, that predicts which ghastly power dispersions are seen because of the reality the indistinguishable shading (see metamerism), however isn't considerably perceptually uniform [1]. The reason toward the rear of CIELAB became to shape a spot that can be registered through honest plan from the CIEXYZ region anyway is extra perceptually uniform than CIEXYZ [2] when putting away shading values abuse restricted accuracy, utilizing a perceptually uniform shading region can upgrade the imitation of tones (Fig. 4).

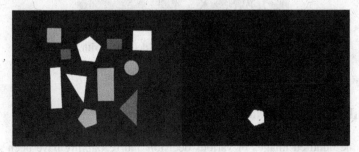

Fig. 4. (Right) The original image. (Left) The masks image for the blue pentagon at the lowest of the photograph, indicating that we can most effectively carry out computations in the "white" vicinity of the photograph, ignoring the black background. (Color figure online)

3.2 Detect the Color

In order to discover the color, we manage loading the photo from disk after which create a resized model of it, maintaining song of the ratio of the unique peak to the resized peak. We then resized the photo in order that our contour approximation is extra correct for form identification. Furthermore, the smaller the photo is, the much less information there may be to process, therefore our code will execute faster. We, then, carried out Gaussian smoothing to our resized photo, changing to grayscale and L*a*b*, and eventually thresh-protecting to expose the shapes within side the photo. We locate the contours (i.e., outlines) of the shapes looking after to seize the best tuple values.

We begin looping over every of the contours, even as computing the middle of the form. Using the contour, we will then stumble on the form of the object, accompanied via way of means of figuring out its color. Finally, we cope with drawing the define of the modern-day form, accompanied via way of means of the color + textual content label at the output image (Fig. 5).

As you can see from the image below, each object has been correctly identified both in terms of shape and in terms of color.

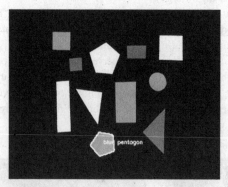

Fig. 5. Shape identification and color detection with labeling.

4 Results and Discussion

A set of one hundred images of various decision and readability have been used for checking out of this set of rules and the consequences have been on the whole accurate. Red, green, blue, magenta, cyan, yellow and white colorings have been efficaciously detected on those photographs. The end result of this detection relies upon on the brink cost that has been set for the photographs. The predominant trouble with thresh-retaining is that it considers simplest depth values of the pixels and does now no longer think about any dating among them. Sometimes greater pixels are detected which are not the part of the favored region, and with growth in noise those mistakes increases. In the technique of labeling of related additives for image segmentation there may be one trouble, that if overlapping items are found in an image, then it'll keep in mind it as simplest one object.

5 Conclusion and Future Work

With the assist of an image processing toolbox in Python, this system was made that can stumble on red, blue, green, magenta, yellow, cyan colors. Also, the colored item is being enclosed inner bounded vicinity alongside the centroid of that vicinity.

1. Computer imaginative and prescient – Color detection is the fundamental and critical step for intending in pc imaginative and prescient. Some unique forms of spectacles may be made to be able to employ pc imaginative and prescient (photo processing) along with neural networks to offer a synthetic imaginative and prescient to blind people.
2. Spy robots – The secret agent robots are made to discover gadgets along-with the vicinity wherein they're launched. Objects' shape, size, color, orientation is of significance to the robot.
3. Object Segregation – An item may be segregated (separated) on the premise of its color.
4. Object Tracking – A transferring item may be tracked on the premise of its color.

References

1. Barni, M.: Document and Image Compression, 1st edn. CRC Press, Boca Raton, USA (2018)
2. Hussain, A.J., Al-Fayadh, A., Radi, N.: Image compression techniques: a survey in lossless and lossy algorithms. Neurocomputing **300**, 44–69 (2018). https://doi.org/10.1016/j.neucom.2018.02.094
3. Nader, J., Alqadi, Z.A., Zahran, B.: Analysis of color image filtering methods. Int. J. Comput. Appl. **174**(8), 12–17 (2017)
4. Khansari, M., Kappler, D., Luo, J., Bingham, J., Kalakrishnan, M.: Action image representation: learning scalable deep grasping policies with zero real world data. In: 2020 IEEE International Conference on Robotics and Automation (ICRA), pp. 3597–3603. IEEE (2020)
5. Jhuo, I., Gao, S., Zhuang, L., Lee, D.T., Ma, Y.: Unsupervised feature learning for RGB-D image classification. In: Cremers, D., Reid, I., Saito, H., Yang, M.-H. (eds.) ACCV 2014. LNCS, vol. 9003, pp. 276–289. Springer, Cham (2015). https://doi.org/10.1007/978-3-319-16865-4_18
6. Kumah, C., Zhang, N., Raji, R.K., Pan, R.: Color measurement of segmented printed fabric patterns in lab color space from RGB digital images. J. Textile Sci. Technol. **5**(1), 1–18 (2019)
7. Qiu, Y., Lu, H., Deng, N., Cai, N.: A robust blind image watermarking scheme based on template in Lab color space. In: Yanwen, Wu. (ed.) ICCIC 2011. CCIS, vol. 234, pp. 402–410. Springer, Heidelberg (2011). https://doi.org/10.1007/978-3-642-24091-1_52
8. Schwarz, M.W., Cowan, W.B., Beatty, J.C.: An experimental comparison of RGB, YIQ, LAB, HSV, and opponent color models. ACM Trans. Graph. **6**(2), 123–158 (1987)

Educational Robot for Assignments Checking

Iqra Yaqoob[✉] and Shahbaz Ahmed

Department of Computer Science, The Islamia University of Bahawalpur, Bahawalpur, Pakistan
iqra.yaqoob@gmail.com

Abstract. Educational robots are used for educating children of all age in science and technology. They are using for delivering education and enhancing cognitive, programming and technical skills in students. A software module is proposed which is helpful in education sector and is helpful for teachers by checking student's assignments. Data file is given to module it will compare student's assignments with it and give result. Given result will show the accuracy of assignment. It will be great time saver for teachers and students will get their assignments checked in time.

Keywords: Cognitive · Automatic assignment marking · Educational robots

1 Introduction

The most emerging technology Robot is a machine that is capable of doing complex task automatically. It is programmed in such a way that it perform many arduous task by giving instructions. Robots that resembles humans are called humanoid robot [1, 2, 5]. They perform task like humans, perform behaviors and actions and are designed artificially intelligent. Humanoid robots are used for research purpose. Moreover, humanoid robots are being developed to perform human tasks like personal assistance, through which they should be able to assist the sick and elderly, and dirty or dangerous jobs [3, 6, 7]. Humanoids are also suitable for some jobs as reception-desk, automotive manufacturing line workers and administrators. In essence, since they can use tools and operate equipment and vehicles designed for the human form. Proper software is required for humanoids to perform any task a human being can. Some robots are using now a days for education purpose these robots are called educational robots. Educational robots are available in a wide range which help to build students cognitive knowledge as well as other skills like programming, mathematics etc. [3, 4]. They are helpful in improving mental skills and are helpful in building teamwork, self-esteem, creativity, self-assessment and practical knowledge. Today there are many educational robots for children and young people. The most popular are mBot, Robo Wunderkind, OWI 535, LEGO Mindstorms EV3, NAO and many more.

The main objective of the research is to develop humanoid educational robot that will be able to help teachers and students in education. Educational robots should include such features that will helpful in educational matters instead of only lecture delivering. For this purpose, we introduce a feature in educational robot that will be helpful for

D. N. A. Jawawi et al. (Eds.): ESMoC 2021, CCIS 1615, pp. 84–90, 2022.
https://doi.org/10.1007/978-3-031-19968-4_9

teachers as well as students. A software module is added in educational robot due to this robot will be able to assist teachers in checking students' assignments. It will be a revolution as it will also maintain quality of education as well as it will be helpful in saving teachers' time.

2 Literature Review

Makeblock mBot is educational robot used for STEAM education and students can learn programming with simple concepts and with fun. Children can learn to build robot by using screwdriver, a manual is given to follow that robot can be easily built. It has advance programming feature. To connect mBot wirelessly with computer you can use Makeblock Bluetooth Dongle. Robo Wunderkind consist of different blocks with tools installed inside them. Children can make nightlight, droid and built a car [13, 14]. Using its app student can guide robot to perform actions like run car, turn on lights etc. it will enhance problem solving skills, teamwork, math logics in children. OWI 535 is a robotic arm kit suitable for young people aged 13 or over. It can lift objects weighing up to 100 g and has a wide variety of movements [10, 12]. This robot is also recommended for vocational training cycles. Students learn by assembling its parts to make arm working. LEGO Mindstorms EV3 is fully functional robot which can walk, talk and can play. This package includes a robotics set that has several sensors for touch and IR. You can download EV3 programmer app to control robot. LEGO Mindstorms come up with 17 different robot designs that can walk, talk and perform many movements. NAO is one of the most popular autonomous and programmable robot. It is suitable for advance STEAM concepts. It has 45 degree of freedom. It is used for research purpose [15, 17]. Due to its attractive interface and shape it is popular among teachers and students. It has the ability to speak, walk and communicate with students.

3 Materials and Methods

In this section, we propose a module in humanoid robot that will check student's assignments and will be a great helper for teachers. It will help in reducing overburdened teachers by checking student's lot of assignments in time and with accuracy. A teacher has to provide all possible answers of given assignments. This module will check data according to data provided by teachers. It will match student assignment data with teachers provided data and will give result.

Figure 1 shows the block diagram of proposed model for assignments checking. Many educational robots are working for learning Science and technology education for students. Proposed model will be an innovation in educational robots. It has several modules working in connection with one another to produce desired output.

3.1 Signal Detection Module

This module is used to detect and receive signals from external world. Sensors are used in it which can easily detect text, image, colors, shapes etc. ASR module Automatic speech recognition ASR module helps robot to produce speech to communicate with external world [11]. ALSpeechRecognition library is used to produce speech.

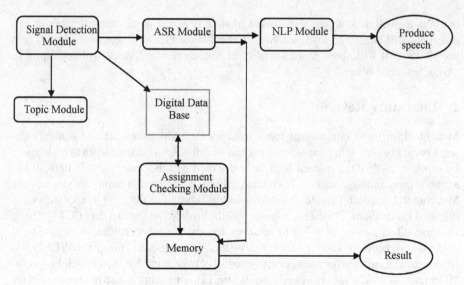

Fig. 1. Software module for assignment checking

3.2 NLP Module

Allows users to speak naturally to their devices. Avoids need to learn restricted command sets. Sensory's TruluNatural is a software development kit which provides speaker independent, large vocabulary continuous speech. It is easy to integrate into applications [16].

3.3 Topic Module

This module has the data provided by teacher about any topic. This data is compared by student's assignment data and marking is done according to this data.

3.4 Digital Data Base

This data base is used to store student's submitted assignments and their record.

3.5 Assignment Checking Module

The algorithm of this module is designed for assignment checking. It will check assignments by comparing with provided data and gives result.

3.6 Memory

This module has record of results of checked assignments which are used for displaying.

The above-mentioned software module has signal detection module to detect assignments submission [8, 9]. That module is notified that all the assignments are submitted now other components must check assignments. Signal detection module get signals for further processing of assignments and pass these signals to ASR module which further pass signals to NLP module to produce speech. Robot will produce speech that all assignments are submitted now it's time to check them. Signal detection module passes signals further to digital data base as well as to topic module. After notifying, topic module will get data from user (teacher) to upload all possible answers of assignment. From signal detection module all assignments data of one type passes to digital data base. It will store data of all assignments of one type (one section). Digital database will send assignment file one by one to assignment checking module from here one by one all assignments will get checked and result will pass to memory module. Memory module will save all checked assignments and their results to display. One by one result of all assignments is displayed on demand of user. Result will give percentage of correct assignment data.

By using this module teachers have not bother to check assignment one by one. This will be a great time saver and students will get their assignments in time as well. Teachers can use this time for some other useful tasks. The result of checked assignments will be stored for further processing if required.

4 Results and Discussion

Main possible answer file was given in .txt format to the assignment checking module that compared student's assignment data and results of 3 sample assignments are shown below:

25 total matches found.
Extending match forwards with words: pray pray
Extending match forwards with words: marry marry
Extending match forwards with words: fervid fervid
Extending match forwards with words: stay stay
Extending match forwards with words: us us

Match 1:
Adams: (12034, 12443) closely, as the first description of Dorothea shows mind was theoretic, and yearned by its nature after some lofty conception of the world which might frankly include the parish of Tipton and her own rule of conduct there; she was enamoured of intensity and greatness, and rash in embracing whatever seemed to her to have those aspects; likely to seek martyrdom, to make retractations, and then to incur martyrdom after all in a quarter where she had not sought central issue of marriage is raised immediately.

Middlemarch: (5809, 6218) interest in gimp and artificial protrusions of drapery mind was theoretic, and yearned by its nature after some lofty conception of the world which might frankly include the parish of Tipton and her own rule of conduct there; she was enamoured of intensity and greatness, and rash in embracing whatever seemed to her to have those aspects; likely to seek martyrdom, to make retractations, and then to incur martyrdom after all in a quarter w here she had not sought Certainly such elements in the character of a marriageable girl.

Match 2:
Adams: (12574, 12694) immediately-"And how should Dorothea not marry?" (p. 6)-with its obvious answer young lady of some birth and fortune, who knelt suddenly down on a brick floor by the side of a sick labourer and prayed fervidly 3George Eliot's "Middlemarch" Notebooks.

Middlemarch: (8751, 8870) might lead her at last to refuse all young lady of some birth and fortune, who knelt suddenly down on a brick floor by the side of a sick laborer and prayed fervidly as if she thought herself living in the time of the Apostles.

Match 3:
Adams: (13292, 13447) org/terms 74 NINETEENTH-CENTURY FICTION thought herself living in the time of the Apostles-who had strange whims of fasting like a Papist, and of sitting up at night to read old theological books Although the parallel relaxes, it remains the organizing.

Middlemarch: (8890, 9046) side of a sick laborer and prayed fervidly thought herself living in the time of the Apostles--who had strange whims of fasting like a Papist, and of sitting up at night to read old theological books wife might awaken you some fine.

Table 1 shows a brief description of the results of software module. It will give almost 90% accurate result by checking assignments. Result will be checked on the base of text matching, proper grammar used and overall answer accuracy by comparing with main data file.

Table 1. Results table

Assignments	Text matching	Grammar	Accuracy
Assignment1	90%	80%	90%
Assignment 2	92%	83%	92%
Assignment 3	85%	83%	85%

A graph in Fig. 2 shows the results.

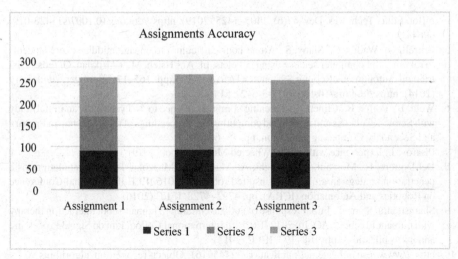

Fig. 2. Results of the study

5 Conclusion

Due to advancement in information technology education sector has a great revolution. The mode of education has become modernized. Teaching methods has changed from classroom lectures to online. Education through humanoid robots is an increasing trend and enable an organization to remain competitive and it is also attractive for students to learn in a new way. Previously many educational robots are working for delivering STEM education to almost all age groups. They are using to teach programming and technology related knowledge to students. No educational robot is used to cover other educational areas such as quiz and viva taking, assignments checking etc. Teachers are burdened with lecture material preparation, quizzes and assignments checking, distance learning lectures etc. Proposed educational humanoid robot is used as a great helper for teachers in assignments checking. A software module is added in humanoid robot that will help teachers by checking student assignments. It will be a great revolution in education sector as it will save time of teachers and students will get their assignments checked in time.

References

1. Gelin, R.: NAO. In: Goswami, A., Vadakkepat, P. (eds.) Humanoid Robotics: A Reference, pp. 1–22. Springer Netherlands, Dordrecht (2018). https://doi.org/10.1007/978-94-007-7194-9_14-1
2. Gouaillier, D., et al.: Mechatronic design of NAO humanoid. In: Robotic and Automation ICRA 2009, pp. 769–774. IEEE, Kobe (2009)
3. Fiorini, P.: Encouraging robotics to take root [teaching tool]. IEEE Robot. Autom. Mag. **12**(3), 15–25 (2005). https://doi.org/10.1109/MRA.2005.1511864
4. Sáez-López, J.-M., Sevillano-García, M.-L., Vazquez-Cano, E.: The effect of programming on primary school students' mathematical and scientific understanding: educational use of

mBot. Educ. Tech. Res. Dev. **67**(6), 1405–1425 (2019). https://doi.org/10.1007/s11423-019-09648-5

5. Correll, N., Wailes, C., Slaby, S.: A one-hour curriculum to engage middle school students in robotics and computer science using cubelets. In: Ani Hsieh, M., Chirikjian, G. (eds.) Distributed Autonomous Robotic Systems. STAR, vol. 104, pp. 165–176. Springer, Heidelberg (2014). https://doi.org/10.1007/978-3-642-55146-8_12

6. Wohl, B., Porter, B., Clinch, S.: Teaching computer science to 5–7 year-olds: an initial study with Scratch, Cubelets and unplugged computing. In: Proceedings of the Workshop in Primary and Secondary Computing Education, pp. 55–60 (2015)

7. Pisarov, J.: Experience with mBot–Wheeled Mobile Robot (2019)

8. Del Dottore, E., Mondini, A., Sadeghi, A., Mattoli, V., Mazzolai, B.: Circumnutations as a penetration strategy in a plant-root-inspired robot. In: 2016 IEEE International Conference on Robotics and Automation (ICRA), pp. 4722–4728. IEEE (2016)

9. Shamsuddin, S., et al.: Initial response of autistic children in human-robot interaction therapy with humanoid robot NAO. In: 2012 IEEE 8th International Colloquium on Signal Processing and its Applications, pp. 188–193. IEEE (2012)

10. https://www.researchgate.net/publication/324459161_Object_recognition_algorithms_implemented_on_NAO_robot_for_children's_visual_learning_enhancement

11. https://www.researchgate.net/publication/259016889_An_Italian_Event-Based_ASRTTS_System_for_the_Nao_Robot

12. Kewalramani, S., et al.: The integration of the internet of toys in early childhood education: a platform for multi-layered interactions. Eur. Early Childh. Educ. Res. J. **28**(2), 197–213 (2020)

13. Kim, H.J., Lee, J.: Designing diving beetle inspired underwater robot (D. BeeBot). In: 2014 13th International Conference on Control Automation Robotics and Vision (ICARCV). IEEE (2014)

14. Papadakis, S.: Robots and Robotics Kits for Early Childhood and First School Age, pp. 34–56 (2020)

15. Hofer, D.P., Strohmeier, F.: Multilingual speech control for ROS-driven robots. Elektrotech. Infech. **136**(7), 334–340 (2019). https://doi.org/10.1007/s00502-019-00739-y

16. Pires, J.N.: Robot-by-voice: experiments on commanding an industrial robot using the human voice. Ind. Robot Int. J. **32**, 505–511 (2004). https://doi.org/10.1108/01439910510629244

17. Chatterjee, K., et al.: Qualitative analysis of POMDPs with temporal logic specifications for robotics applications. In: 2015 IEEE International Conference on Robotics and Automation (ICRA). IEEE (2015)

Detection and Prevention COVID- 19 Patients Using IoT and Blockchain Technology

Israr Ahmad[✉], Adeel Ahmed, and Saima Abdullah

Department of Computer Science, The Islamia University of Bahawalpur, Bahawalpur, Pakistan
rao_israr@yahoo.com

Abstract. COVID-19 epidemic second wave is affecting the world severely. It is a gigantic challenge for governments of all countries to protect their citizens from this virus and put effected ones in quarantine centers so that these can't cause of spreading Covid-19 virus any more. There is no trustworthy treatment of this disease till now (16 November 2020). Complete Lockdown is not solution for this pandemic because this can lead heavy loss of economy and can cause enhance in poverty and hunger in society. In this study we proposed a smart method of detection and prevention the people from COVID-19 with help of IoT and Blockchain technologies. Now a day's sensor is a cheap technology and different devices can be thru sensors. Each person in COVID-19 suspected area has a smart corona belt in his wrest along with face mask. This belt consists of different hardware modules like sensors, tiny battery and transvers. Sensors collect the different symptoms of a person for COVID-19 then this information will be communicated to other entities like government database, quarantine center and rescue office. This corona belt can detect a person as safe, suspected, high Suspected and positive. A person is safe if he has no COVID-19 symptoms and also not met someone having COVID-19 positive. If someone has COVID-19 symptoms then he is suspected case and if someone has COVID-19 symptoms and also met with COVID-19 positive he will be high Suspected case. All smart corona belts communicate with cellular phone running COVID-19 application for processing and sending messages to government database, corona centre and rescue centers for different actions. In this proposed solution three layered architecture is used to enhance the flexibility and effectiveness of system. The whole process is enabled by IoT, fog and cloud technologies. All information is stored using blockchain for the sake of data privacy, Integrity and security.

Keywords: COVID-19 · Corona Virus · IoT · Fog networks · Cloud networks · Blockchain

1 Introduction

According to the world health organization (WHO) a pandemic is the spread of a new disease worldwide [1]. A more elaborated definition of the pandemic says: an epidemic occurring worldwide or over a vast area, crossing international boundaries and usually affecting all peoples across the countries [2]. On March 11, 2020, the WHO has

© Springer Nature Switzerland AG 2022
D. N. A. Jawawi et al. (Eds.): ESMoC 2021, CCIS 1615, pp. 91–100, 2022.
https://doi.org/10.1007/978-3-031-19968-4_10

announced the outbreak of novel coronavirus disease (COVID-19 or SARS-CoV-2) a pandemic [3] and as of November 16, 2020, 07:40 PM Pakistan standard time, there has been 54.4 million confirmed cases across the world according to WHO Coronavirus disease (COVID-19) [4]. However, an outburst of coronavirus infection may be spread in real if the safety measure like quarantine and isolation of the infected or exposed peoples are not applying. To minimize the growth of infections quarantine along with the isolation and social distancing plays an important role [5]. According to the WHO has defined the quarantine of persons is the restrictions of activities and separation from other persons who are not ill but who may be outburst to an infectious disease, to monitor the symptoms and detection of the early infection. Introducing quarantine measures early in a disease outbreak delay the infectious disease outbreak and delay the peak of an epidemic in a country [6].

The tracking of the COVID-19 is carried out through mobile applications, thermal cameras, and IoT for detection and prevention. The IoT originally referred to as frequency identification technology and device mutual with the internet based on the agreed transmission protocol to achieve intelligent management of agent information. Moreover, this idea has been explored and expanded, that is the use of smart grid sensor devices used with internet to connect peoples to people and machine to peoples. The most reliable features of the IoT is the ubiquitous computing, intellectual processing, widespread sensitivity [7, 8]. Blockchain is a growing list of records called a block of the storage data in the Blockchain repository. These blocks connected using cryptography. With the invention of the Blockchain technology elimination of the centralization, architecture is overcome. Blockchain provides excellent features such as transparency, decentralization architecture, and tamper-proof system, which is most valuable for the data transmission from IoT based devices to Edge and fog architectures. Today Blockchain is using for the secure service provisioning and data sharing for the satisfaction of the client. Mostly existing Blockchain technologies for IoT devices cause low latency, low throughput, and network delay like issue while data transmission over the wireless link.

Motivating by these existing systems, we proposed a secure service provisioning rescue belt for the COVID-19 detection and prevention Blockchain-based architecture for health care. The smart belt having the capability of sensor communication and battery module to forward the exposed COVID-19 personal to the health care center immediately to delay the outbreak of the infectious disease in the reported area. The belt will sense personal symptoms and can communicate with other people belt and can communicate with an edge server than edge server will provide required service to the requested rescue belt personal by requesting from the cloud layer which is integrated with Blockchain foe secure service provisioning for secure data transmission between the health data center the agent or client belt. Due to Blockchain technologies, secure service provisioning of COVID-19 exposed personal and secure edge computing devices is possible. Blockchain technology involvement eliminates the risk of malicious activity and data transmission from the fake COVID-19 belt and personal.

2   Related Work

The epidemic of novel coronavirus (COVID-19) that started in Wuhan, China, seems to be unstoppable across the boundaries of all countries. An outburst of this unknown disease started in Wuhan, Hubei province in China in 2019. The world now is struggling to control the epidemic virus, since there is no specific treatment for the novel coronavirus. So, there is an urgent need for global surveillance of the peoples exposed with active COVID-19 infectious disease. The affluence of new technology IoT which gaining global attention for prediction, prevention, and monitoring of novel infectious diseases, data privacy has become an important concern regarding the potential for data misuse and abuse. This research proposed IoT and related technologies for smart disease surveillance system for simultaneous reporting, monitoring, end to end connectivity, data analysis, tracking, and alerts, as well as for remote medical assistance to exposed COVID-19 personal [9]. The world health organization (WHO) has declared the novel COVID-19 coronavirus disease a pandemic. The exposed person at quarantine subjects is a more serious concern for the other peoples present there. As the literature suggests a wearable can help to detect and prevent infectious disease to delay outbursts these pandemics. This research designed an IoT based wearable quarantine band (IoT-Q-Band) to detect COVID-19 exposed personal, designed by keeping in mind the cost, global supply chain, and COVID-19 quarantine duration, which the WHO recommends [10].

The year 2020 should have been the start of an exciting era in the health care sector, with the development of many digital technologies that can be used to tackle, diagnose, monitor major clinical problems and infectious diseases. These digital technologies include the IoT, with next generation telecommunication networks (5G) big data, artificial intelligence integration with the deep learning and Blockchain, using for clinical detection and prevention for infectious disease such as COVID-19 [11].

One of the major symptoms of the COVID-19 that can be easily detected and identified easily is fever. This study proposes the design of the system that can identify the coronavirus automatically from a thermal image with low human involvement using IoT based smart helmet with mounted Thermal Imaging System for the pandemic disease [12].

In [13] the main aim of the authors is to design a system without human interaction to detect coronavirus automatically from the fast-thermal image using IoT based drone technology. Furthermore, the proposed system having the capability for using virtual reality, so the living scanning process will be monitored through the VR screen to make it a reality and less human interaction to detect infectious disease such as COVID-19.

2.1 Blockchain in IoT

In [14] authors designed a hybrid network for the smart cities combining the two emerging technologies Blockchain technology and the software-defined network (SDN). To achieve maximum throughput, the authors divided the network into two parts such as the core network and the edge network.

Oscar in [15] presents a proof of concept mechanism using Blockchain for access management in IoT. Other states of the art management access system also evaluated in this article. However, the system proposed in this research is much scalable when the load is distributed.

2.2 Blockchain in WSN

In [16] the author's presents of Rolling Blockchain for wireless sensor networks (WSN) and limitation of the WSN model how to implement wireless sensor networks connects with Blockchain. Furthermore, it is different from the network denser, node failure will be less affected, but if the network is less dense than some node failure may cause the network to break down.

In [17] the two emerging technologies Blockchain and artificial intelligence are implemented combine to design secure data sharing. In this research both the data chain and behavior chain is combining to get a secure mechanism for secure data transmission.

Currently much emphasis is given on the integration of cloud, fog and edge infrastructure with IoT to support its execution and intensive computing applications. Many real-world frameworks attempt to assist such integration concerning platform independence, security, resource management, and multiple application execution. This research proposed an integration framework named fog Bus that facilities end to end IoT fog (Edge) cloud integration, it helps developers to build IoT applications also helps users to run multiple applications at the same time and manage their resources [18].

3 System Architecture

There are number of proposed architectures for IoT system in literature. Three-layered architecture is more flexible and provide enhanced performance. Our system based on three layered architecture. The first layer is IoT layer or device layer second is fog layer and third is cloud layer. Next question is which layer is most suitable for blockchain integration. In this solution we integrate blockchain at cloud layer because at first layer limited resource smart corona belt is used and it is not possible to apply blockchain configuration at this layer. Mobile devices are used at fog layer and resources required for blockchain can not be supported the cell phones. Due to these constraints, cloud is used for blockchain implementation in this solution as shown in Fig. 1.

Fig. 1. System architecture

First layer consist of IoT devices in our case IoT devices are smart corona belt which get information from user symptoms also from surrounding and sends information to cellular phone to which this belt is directly connected. Second layer is fog layer which is introduced to minimize the response time and bring the processing near to data generation. Last is cloud layer used to implement blockchain to store the transactions.

4 Proposed Solution

COVID-19 is a pandemic spreading in whole world without respect of boundaries, nations, state and religion. An effected person can spread this virus to healthier ones. This pandemic has some common symptoms like cough, fever and flu. Some patients my feel some other symptoms also beside common ones like headache, pain in body, blood pressure disturbance and trouble in breathing. Diagnostic process of COVID-19 is not simple and fast. It takes at least 48 h in developing countries like Pakistan and India. These developing countries have not so much resources to diagnose a large population of the country. In this paper we use the IoT and blockchain technologies to detect someone having chance of COVID-19 positive. The people in area where this pandemic is spreading will have smart corona belt in their wrest. This belt has sensors that can sense different symptoms in a person like fever and cough and flu also communicate with the cloud. This belt has a rechargeable battery source.

COVID-19 has paralyzed world economy but we have to survive such situations. Business activities has to started and keep safe ourselves as well. So, we have to take help of technology to do so. The people of the area where the pandemic has spread or likely to spread use cheap corona belt equipped with sensors, transvers and battery module have to use. This belt may be connected to some cellular phone or can work autonomously. Corona belt sense the person symptoms and communicate with sink for further processing. There are four configurations of belt, first is safe when the person has neither symptoms nor met with someone has COVID-19 positive. Secondly suspected case, if a person has symptoms or met someone has COVID-19 positive. Thirdly, highly suspected when some person has COVID-19 symptoms and met someone having COVID-19 positive. Fourth is COVID-19 positive this configuration is associated with laboratory verification (Fig. 2).

Fig. 2. Smart corona belt

A person having Corona belt can perform business activities and can safe itself with corona virus. If a person is in COVID-19 safe mode green light on belt will turn on and after verifying green light status may be allowed to enter in shopping mall or in hall for some activity. If someone is in safe state and found suspected, highly suspected or positive case in surroundings, his belt will give alert to take appropriate precautions like social distancing. If someone is in suspected state the red light will be turn on and green light switch off and in case of highly suspected state two red lights will be turn on. In case of suspected and highly suspected case a message and location in sent to nearly corona center and rescue office. He or she can bring in corona center for laboratory verifications. In case found COVID-19 positive bring him/her in quarantine center for treatment otherwise given medicines of diagnostic illness and his belt status will turn to green indicate safe state and permit to go home.

5   Technical Aspect

Each corona belt consists of three hardware modules sensors sense the symptoms, transceiver to communicated sensed data and battery resources for energy to the belt. There are three types of sensors in a belt for temperature, cough and flu (Fig. 3).

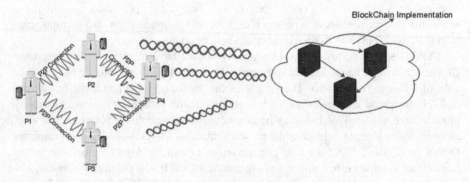

Fig. 3. Proposed network

Communication hardware module consists of a Bluetooth device which can communicate with cell phone which is running an application to handle the whole process. The belt can embed with Wi-Fi capabilities for communication directly with cloud which can increase per belt cost. In this case we will use Bluetooth capabilities connected with cellular phone also we can take benefits of fog computing with this integration. The smart phone having Wi-Fi, 4G or 5G connection is used to carry message till cloud. To take benefits of privacy, integrity and security all data is stored in blockchain on cloud.

Each person has cellular phone and smart corona belt connected each other through Bluetooth connection and configured with application running on phone. Cell phone has two connections first for Peer to Peer (P2P) and second for cloud. Smart corona belt sense user symptoms and send message to cell phone which take appropriate action and send message to cloud if found Suspected or high Suspected and store in a block of blockchain. If found safe state keep green light on.

```
1: IF sensor state change
2:      Bluetooth Connection ON
3: ELSE
4:      Bluetooth Connection OFF
5: END IF
6: IF temp> Threshold OR Cough=True OR flu=True
7:      Send Message Suspected
8: END IF
9: IF Meet with Person Corona Positive= True
10:      Send Message Suspected
11: END IF
12: IF Suspectable=True AND Meet with COVID-19 Positive=True
13:      Send Message Highly Suspected
14: END IF
15: IF Message = "Suspected"
16:      Turn on First Red light
17:        MultiCast_Message()
18: End IF
19: IF Message = "Highly Suspected"
20:      Turn on First two Red light
21:        MultiCast_Message()
22: End IF
23: IF Lab Verification Positive =True
24:      Turn On third Red Light
25:        Send message (Transaction) to the Cloud (Blockchain)
as Positive
26:      Assign bed in Quarantine Center
27: ELSE
28:      Turn on Green Light
29:        Send message (Transaction) to the Cloud (Blockchain)
as Negative
30:      Give Medicines
31: END IF
32: Function MultiCast_Message()
33:   \  Send message and Location to Corona Center
34:      Send Message and Location to Rescue office
35:        Send message (Transaction) to
the Cloud (Blockchain)  36: END Function
```

Line 1–5: Corona belt is powered by tiny battery source to preserve the energy Bluetooth connection between belt and cellular phone is not permanent only if sensors have some new event then connection becomes active otherwise in sleep mode. Line 6–8: If belt measures some symptoms like fever, cough or flu then it sends message to cell phone "suspected". Line 9–11: If someone having COVID-19 positive state and within its radio range for specific time period it also sends "Suspected" message to cell phone application. Line 12–14: If two conditions are met simultaneously first COVID-19 positive is in its radio range and COVID-19 symptoms found.

"Highly Suspected" message is sent to phone. Line 15–18: If phone application receive.

"Suspected" message from belt, it turn on first red light on belt also Multi-cast_Message() function is called which send three message first in corona center with patient location. When corona center receives message, it takes appropriate arrangement for his/her like testing. Second message with location is sent to rescue office to bring patient to corona center. Third message with location is sent to Government database where this transaction is stored on cloud in a clock if blockchain. Line 19–22: When highly suspected message is received to cell application it turns on two red lights and send three messages as in line 15–18. Line 23–31: If Laboratory verified the patient as COVID-19 positive third red light on belt is turn on and message is sent to cloud where information about patient is stored on blockchain and bed in quarantine center. If patient is found negative green light on belt is turn on and message is sent to cloud as negative where information of patient is stored on Blockchain and medicines is given about symptoms. Line 32–36: A message sending function is define in which three messages is sent on three station as mentioned above (Fig. 4).

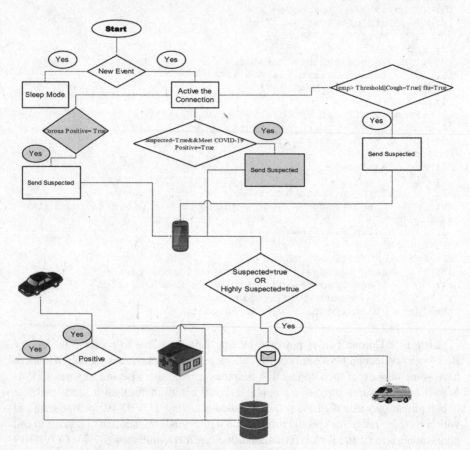

Fig. 4. Dataflow diagram

6   Conclusion and Future Work

Computer science and Information Technology is enabling technologies for a lot of medical application like for diagnostics and patient treatment. In this solution we proposed a novel idea of COVID-19 detection and prevention. In this idea a combination of IoT, Fog computing, cloud computing and blockchain is used in three layered architecture. People having smart corona belt and cellular phone is first layer. Smart corona belt senses the COVID-19 symptoms and send it to second layer. A cell phone having COVID application act as fog layer for quick response at second layer. Application can decide a person as safe, suspected, highly suspected or positive. When a person is detected as suspected or highly suspected then application multicast three message with location of suspected person to government database, corona center and reuse office for quick response. In this solution patient data is stored in blockchain for data integrity and privacy of patient. Currently client server architecture is used for such solutions.

In future we will simulate different scenarios of proposed idea to show the reliability and correctness through generated results. This idea will be enhanced for other medical applications. After the success of this idea a smart ring will be introduced for some common disease like hart patients to detect the patient condition in real time and patient data will be stored in Blockchain. Currently number of applications are being used all are based on client server model and vulnerable to different types of attack like Denial of Server attack. After implementing this new idea data privacy and integrity can be maintained easily.

References

1. Lee, K.: World Health Organization. Edward Elgar Publishing, In Handbook of Governance and Security (2014)
2. Kelly, H.: The classical definition of a pandemic is not elusive. Bull. World Health Organ. **89**, 540–541 (2011)
3. Grasselli, G., et al.: Baseline Characteristics and Outcomes of 1591 Patients Infected with SARS-CoV-2 Admitted to ICUs of the Lombardy Region, Italy. JAMA - Journal of the American Medical Association (2020). https://doi.org/10.1001/jama.2020.5394
4. American Nurses Association: Coronavirus Disease (COVID-19). American Nurses Credentialing Center, March 2020, 1–7 (2020). https://www.nursingworld.org/practice-policy/workenvironment/health-safety/disaster-preparedness/coronavirus/
5. Wilder-Smith, A., Freedman, D.O.: Isolation, quarantine, social distancing, and community containment: Pivotal role for old-style public health measures in the novel coronavirus (2019-nCoV) outbreak. J. Travel Med. **27**(2), 1–4 (2020). https://doi.org/10.1093/jtm/taaa020
6. WHO: Considerations for quarantine of individuals in the context of containment for coronavirus disease (COVID-19). Who, February, 3–5 (2020)
7. National Health Commission of the People's Republic of China: Laboratory biosafety guide for 2019-nCoV (Second Edition). Biosafety and Health **2**(1), 1–2 (2020). https://doi.org/10.1016/j.bsheal.2020.01.001
8. Song, Y., Jiang, J., Wang, X., Yang, D., Bai, C.: Prospect and application of internet of things technology for prevention of SARIs. Clinical EHealth **3**, 1–4 (2020). https://doi.org/10.1016/j.ceh.2020.02.001

9. Bai, L., et al.: Chinese experts' consensus on the Internet of Things-aided diagnosis and treatment of coronavirus disease 2019 (COVID-19). Clinical EHealth **3**, 7–15 (2020). https://doi.org/10.1016/j.ceh.2020.03.001

10. Singh, V.K., Chandna, H., Kumar, A., Kumar, S.: EAI endorsed transactions IoT-Q-Band: a low cost internet of things based wearable band to detect and track absconding COVID-19 quarantine subjects. July 2018 (2020). https://doi.org/10.4108/eai.13-7-2018.163997

11. Ting, D.S.W., Carin, L., Dzau, V., Wong, T.Y.: Digital technology and COVID-19. Nat. Med. (2020). https://doi.org/10.1038/s41591-020-0824-5

12. Mohammed, M.N., Syamsudin, H., Al-Zubaidi, S., Sairah, A.K., Ramli, R., Yusuf, E.: Novel Covid-19 Detection and Diagnosis System Using Iot Based Smart Helmet. International Journal of Psychosocial Rehabilitation **24**(7), 2296–2303 (2020). https://doi.org/10.37200/IJPR/V24I7/PR270221

13. Mohammed, M.N., Hazairin, N.A., Al-zubaidi, S.S., Sairah, A.K., Mustapha, S., Yusuf, E.: Toward a novel design for coronavirus detection and diagnosis toward a novel design for coronavirus detection and diagnosis system using Iot based drone technology. International Journal of Psychosocial Rehabilitation **24**(7), 2287–2295 (2020). https://doi.org/10.37200/IJPR/V24I7/PR270220

14. Sharma, P.K., Park, J.H.: Blockchain based hybrid network architecture for the smart city. Futur. Gener. Comput. Syst. **86**, 650–655 (2018). https://doi.org/10.1016/j.future.2018.04.060

15. Novo, O.: Scalable access management in IoT using blockchain: A performance evaluation. IEEE Internet Things J. **6**(3), 4694–4701 (2019). https://doi.org/10.1109/JIOT.2018.2879679

16. Kushch, S., Prietocastrillo, F.: A Rolling Blockchain for a Dynamic WSNs in a Smart City (2018). ArXiv: Cryptography and Security, 1–8. https://es.arxiv.org/abs/1806.11399

17. Zhang, G., Li, T., Li, Y., Hui, P., Jin, D.: Blockchain-based data sharing system for AI-powered network operations. J. Comm. Info. Netw. **3**(3), 1–8 (2018). https://doi.org/10.1007/s41650-018-0024-3

18. Tuli, S., Mahmud, R., Tuli, S., Buyya, R.: FogBus: A blockchain-based lightweight framework for edge and fog computing. J. Syst. Softw. **154**, 22–36 (2019). https://doi.org/10.1016/j.jss.2019.04.050

Vehicle Recognition Using Multi-level Deep Learning Models

Aqsa Hassan, Mohsin Ali, M. Nouman Durrani[⊠], and M. A. Tahir

National University of Computer and Emerging Science, FAST School of Computing,
NUCES-FAST, Karachi, Pakistan
{aqsa.hassan,mohsin.ali,muhammad.nouman,atif.tahir}@nu.edu.pk

Abstract. In the past few years, traditional automatic license plate recognition (ALPR) has received great attention to detect unauthorized vehicles by validating their registration numbers. However, fake license plates have made this task more challenging. This paper introduces a multi-level system to deal with the problem of fake license plates using computer vision and deep learning techniques to extract several other important features such as vehicle color, make and model along with the license plate recognition, which can be beneficial in detecting the illegal vehicles. It can be used by security and law enforcement agencies since stolen vehicles or those used in terrorist and robbery activities normally have a fake license plate attached to them. YOLOv3 is applied for vehicle type detection (i.e. car, motorcycle, bus, truck) while an efficient approach for the license plate text recognition has also been implemented. Make and model recognition of a vehicle using ResNet-152 and Xception are the novel contribution in this paper as these deep learning architectures have never been investigated in this context. Different convolutional neural networks (CNNs) are trained and tested using the Stanford Cars-196 dataset where Xception outperformed previous approaches with 96.7% accuracy. A novel deep neural network for vehicle color recognition has also been introduced in this paper, which is not only computationally inexpensive but also outperforms other competitive methods on the vehicle color dataset.

Keywords: Vehicle make and model recognition · Neural networks · KNN · Vehicle color recognition

1 Introduction

Car theft is an issue of increasing concern as unauthorized vehicles are mainly involved in a large number of illegal activities including street crimes and even terrorist activities [1]. In big cities, this issue is more critical, as millions of vehicles are running on the roads and make it impossible to detect an unauthorized vehicle. In this regard, theft car surveillance is important to help law enforcement agencies and traffic surveillance management systems to ensure better security for their citizens. In literature, researchers have considered traditional license plate recognition as an essential element of the Intelligent Transport System (ITS) [2]. License plate detection and character recognition are mainly involved in the automatic license plate detection and recognition system for validating

© Springer Nature Switzerland AG 2022
D. N. A. Jawawi et al. (Eds.): ESMoC 2021, CCIS 1615, pp. 101–113, 2022.
https://doi.org/10.1007/978-3-031-19968-4_11

vehicle registration numbers. Traffic police use only number plate recognition as an identification tool for tracking stolen vehicles. Since fake license plates are used to hide the identity of stolen and unregistered vehicles, it makes it difficult to recognize those illegal vehicles. As part of the theft car surveillance, number plate recognition cannot be used as a reliable approach for the identification of illegal vehicles. Therefore, we need a system that can identify vehicles other than the traditional vehicle license plate recognition methods. In this work, we proposed a multi-level system that extracts other features such as vehicle color, make, and model at different levels using computer vision and deep learning techniques to identify illegal vehicles on roads. Though in the research literature, separate systems have been proposed for vehicle detection, automatic license plate detection, and recognition, make and model recognition, and color classification but these different components are not combined. To the best of our knowledge, this is the first work that integrates all these systems to identify unauthorized vehicles using multi-level feature extraction. Besides that, we have also investigated several other state-of-the-art CNN architectures in an effort to establish a new baseline for vehicle make and model recognition. The main contributions of this paper are outlined as follows:

1. YOLO v3 [3] has been used for the detection of vehicles and to detect their license plates. This method was initially investigated by Redmon, Joseph et al. in their prior work on object detection. The same approach was recently investigated by Laroca et al. [4] for number plate recognition in an unconstrained environment and we have employed a similar [5] approach in this paper. For license plate rectification to improve the accuracy of OCR, WPOD-NET has been employed. The positive and rectified license plate detected regions are then used by the Optical Character Recognition (OCR) for final character recognition. The same work was also explored by Montazzolli Silva et al. and Shapiro et al. [6]. Finally, we have also compared this approach with another more efficient method for automatic license plate detection and recognition.
2. Make and model detection using ResNet-152 [20] and Xception [22] which are novel contributions in this paper as these models have never been investigated for the vehicle make and model recognition. We have also provided a comparison with the recent deep neural networks to establish a new baseline that outperformed the previous methods for vehicle make and model recognition.
3. Initially, k-NN [7] classifier was implemented for vehicle color recognition. However, a novel deep neural network for color recognition has been introduced in this paper which is more accurate and computationally inexpensive for this task.

The layout of this paper is organized as follows: In Sect. 2, a literature review of recent work related to vehicle detection and recognition systems has been discussed. Section 3 presents the proposed system, followed by the methodology in Sect. 4. Details of experimental setup and datasets are given in Sect. 5 and evaluation and results are discussed in Sect. 6. The overall conclusion is given in Sect. 7.

2   Literature Review

To identify stolen vehicles, traffic police generally use a license plate as a tool. In literature, much work has been done while addressing different approaches for ALPR, the use of license plate recognition for the identification of illegal vehicles is not sufficient because fake license plates have made this task more challenging [4, 5]. Defined ALPR as a three-stage process, namely, license plate extraction, character segmentation, and character recognition. Silva and C. R. Jung [5] proposed an automatic license plate recognition framework capable of detecting and rectifying multiple distorted license plates due to oblique views. In the license plate recognition systems, the detection of the license plate region plays an essential role. In this regard, Silva and C. R. Jung proposed the WPODNET model for accurate license plate detection. This model regresses one affine transformation per detection to rectify the area of LP to a rectangle-like region in a frontal view. The model fed the rectified image to an OCR for the character recognition on a detected license plate. Then the character segmentation and recognition is performed using a modified YOLO network. Their system was accurate on highly distorted LPs, however, it was miss-classifying characters in particular few cases. The same architecture was also investigated by Redmon, et al. [3]. In literature, methods like edge statistics and morphology [11–13] were also commonly used for license plate detection. For an image size 384 × 288, these systems meet the requirement of real-time processing (<47.9 ms) with an accuracy around 97% on extremely small datasets (with < 3k images) [15–17].

Yang et al. [14] worked on the car features analysis due to the lack of highquality datasets availability. They collected a huge dataset (with 50000 images) named "compcar", and used it to carry out classification, verification, and attribute prediction. They used a pre-trained neural network on the ImageNet dataset and further fine-tuned that model using the vehicle images for classification and vehicle attribute prediction. Later on, the fine-tuned model was employed as a feature extractor for vehicle model verification. Though CNN and Joint Bayesian, they achieved an accuracy of 80% and 76.1% on medium, easy and hard levels of difficulties of test datasets respectively. Tafazzoli [9] created a subset dataset (VMMRdb-3036), containing 3036 classes (i.e. only those classes were included which contained more than 20 images) from the original VMMRdb dataset. The model was then trained on VMMRdb-3036 using ResNet-50, and VGG. The model trained using the VMMRdb-3036 dataset achieved the accuracy of 51.76% and 92.90% in top-1 and top-5 metrics respectively.

Rachmadi et al. [18] used CNN for learning classification based on color distribution. In this method, VGG based CNN architectures were used to convert input images to two different color spaces, HSV and CIE Lab. They used the publicly available car dataset [10] containing 15,601 vehicle images for training their proposed model. One similar approach was also investigated on the same dataset by Zhang [8], using deep CNN while adjusting network structure and optimizing network parameters. These approaches were good in obtaining accurate results in normal conditions, however, experienced an increased error rate in nonuniform outdoor illumination conditions and backgrounds.

3 Proposed System

As discussed earlier, separate systems have been proposed for automatic license plate detection and recognition, vehicle make and model recognition, and vehicle color recognition. However, this is the first work that has integrated all these features in a system, We believe that the recognition of license plates plays an important role but it not enough, and if license plate recognition is used with the extraction of a vehicle's other physical features such as make, model, color, and shape. It could help in identifying stolen vehicles more efficiently. Therefore, the proposed system has the following objectives as listed below;

(a) Detection of type of the vehicle (i.e. car, motorcycle, bus, truck).
(b) Detection and recognition of the license plate
(c) Recognition of vehicle manufacturing year, make and it's model
(d) Recognition of vehicle color
(e) Finally, matching the extracted features with a centralized database toverify the authenticity

Initially, the system detects the type of the vehicle and the region of its license plate from a sequence of frames as shown in Fig. 1. For this purpose, we performed transfer-learning using the license plate dataset on YOLOv3 which was pertained on the ImageNet dataset [3]. The outputs of the Warped Planar Object Detection Network (Wpod-Net) which is capable of rectifying distorted license plates of the extracted vehicle are used by the OCR for character recognition of vehicle license plate. This approach was successful in recognizing distorted number plates but unfortunately, misclassifying a few characters (i.e. I as 1 and M as N). Therefore, we have also implemented another more efficient approach for license plate text recognition. Furthermore, to check the authenticity of the license plate we also extracted other important features namely the vehicle color, make and model. In this respect, we first investigated ResNet-152 [25] for the make and model recognition. The model was trained using the Stanford Car-196 dataset which consists of 196 different classes of make and model and contains 16,185 images. To improve the model performance, we used data augmentation on the training dataset in the form of rotation, scaling, and lighting. The Stanford Car dataset was trained with a split of 50% for training and 50% for testing. We have also trained and tested several promising CNNs on the same dataset and Xception [22] has been found to improve the achieved accuracy by 13% on the testing dataset and outperformed other state-of-the-art models such as DenseNet-161 and ResNet152 as shown in Table 1. To recognize the color of the vehicle, initially, we used the k-nearest neighbor which is trained on five major colors i.e. black, white, red, blue, and yellow according to their respective RGB values. Later, we developed a novel CNN for vehicle color recognition which is more accurate and time-efficient as compared to the KNN approach. Finally, these extracted features of the vehicle are matched with the license plate number already stored in a city centralized database to check the authenticity of the vehicle with its registration details as shown in Fig. 1.

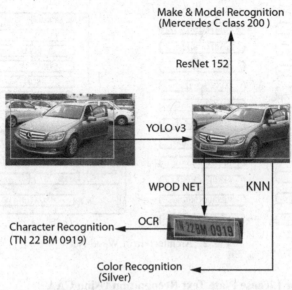

Fig. 1. In first part vehicle detection is done by YOLO v3 which is followed by license plate detection using WPOD-Net along with it model and make recognition is done by Res-Net 152/Xception and color recognition is done by using CNN.

4 Methodology

The proposed system is presented in Fig. 1. In the first part of the system, vehicle type detection and its license plate detection have been performed by YOLO v3 which is followed by license plate rectification by using WPOD-Net.

The output of this model is then used by an OCR for the final character recognition on the license plate. For the make and model recognition, we first investigated ResNet152 and later found xception to outperformed other existing methods where-else color recognition has been performed by using KNN and Convolutional Neural Network. Furthermore, these extracted features are used to validate the vehicle authentication with the help of a city centralized database that already contained the vehicle details of all the registered vehicles i.e. make and model, shape, color, etc.

4.1 The License Plate Recognition Using Wpod-Net

The license plate recognition system involves the three stages namely vehicle detection, license plate detection, and correction, OCR. In this approach, we have used a pre-trained model named WPOD-Net to extract the plate image and its respective coordinates from a vehicle image. Wpod-Net is capable of detecting multiple license plates in one frame but we employed this model to detect only one single license plate from each image. The input image first uses YOLOv3 for vehicle detection, the detected vehicle image is re-entered into the Wpod-Net network to correct the regression of the system, then correct the license plate and input it to the OCR-Net network to identify the license plate characters.

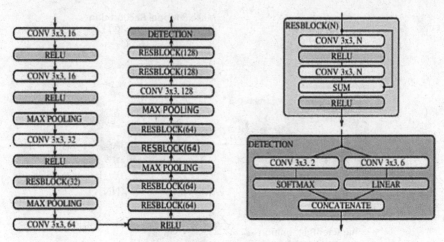

Fig. 2. Architecture of Wpod-Net

4.2 Method for License Plate Text Recognition Using CAA

The above discussed method was useful to detect the distorted license plates but when we tested this model on our internal dataset, we found that it was not accurate as shown in Fig. 3. Therefore, we adopted a more efficient approach for License plate recognition. A high-resolution photographic camera is used to capture vehicle images. However, the characters on the vehicle license plate can become distorted due to the obliqueness of the camera. To solve this problem, a better camera with more definition and resolution will improve the performance of the system. Another method for increasing the success ratio is to employ preprocessing algorithm that involves the resizing of the image to a feasible aspect ratio because the images acquired from a camera might be large. Secondly, the images are generally either in raw format or encoded into some multimedia standards which are captured using IR or photographic cameras. Therefore, the images are converted to grayscale. Finally, the characters are highlighted and the background is suppressed by segmentation using a certain threshold ratio to make the characters and the plate edges bold. This also helps to eliminate the effect of the illumination that appears on the license plates. License plate localization is the stage where the position of the license plate is determined. The input at this stage is a preprocessed image of the vehicle and the output is the license plate. We extracted the license plate using the concept of connected component analysis.

The output images revealed that those regions were also mapped which did not contain the license plate. To eliminate such regions, we used the characteristics knowledge of a typical license plate i.e. they are rectangular in shape, its height is smaller than width, the license plate region is only between 15% and 40% of the width of the full vehicle image, and the proportion of the height of the license plate region to the full image is 8% and 20%. After extracting the license plate, we segmented the license plate into individual characters and then recognized the segmented character respectively using a classifier. Segmentation algorithms mainly consisted of connected component-based. After the segmentation, template matching-based and learning-based algorithms are

Fig. 3. Incorrect/correct outputs using WPOD-NET (i.e. some characters are misclassified in first four license plates images)

used to tackle this character-level classification task. We have implemented a template matching-based algorithm whereas KNN is used for matching.

4.3 The Make and Model Recognition

To validate the authenticity of the vehicle, as part of the theft car surveillance, we also worked on the make and model recognition. Initially, Res-Net 152 [25] was trained on the Stanford car dataset with a split 50–50 (with 100 epochs) to recognize the vehicle make and model. For make and model, the same dataset was trained with a split of 50–50 to recognize the car make and model using ResNet 18. But, in that case, the accuracy was just 65.29% due to the fact, the model is not much deep. However, when we worked on ResNet152, which was a deeper network with 152 residual layers, the system outperformed with 81.37% accuracy. To further improve the obtained results we used the annotations of bounding boxes for both training and test dataset which has resulted in 92% accuracy through fine-tuning. Several CNNs architectures were trained and tested using the same dataset in an effort to establish a new baseline for extended research in the area. Later, Xception was investigated using the same dataset and found to outperform other deep learning models with an accuracy of 96.45% as shown above in Table 1. The results also revealed that Xception not only outperformed other state-of-the-art CNNs for image classification but also among the models with fewer parameters.

Table 1. Comparison of different deep learning models on the Stanford Cars-196 dataset.

Model	Accuracy
ResNet-18	65.29%
VGG [24]	86.8%
ResNet-152 [27]	92%
Inception-v4 [23]	90.5%
Inception-ResNet-v2	91.3%
Xception [22]	**96.45%**
DenseNet-161 [25]	89.7%
MobileNet-v1 [26]	87.6%
DenseNet-121	91.3%

4.4 Vehicle Color Recognition

In order to recognize the color of the vehicle, we have implemented two different approaches. Firstly, we have adopted a model based on k-nearest neighbor which was trained on five major colors i.e. black, white, red, blue, and yellow according to their respective RBG values. This method was giving accurate outputs but it was computationally expensive. Hence, a novel CNN for vehicle color recognition which is more accurate and time-efficient as compared to the KNN approach was developed. This model consists of twenty-one convolutional layers, among which six are convolutional 2d layers, six max-pooling layers, seven activation layers out of which 6 uses 'relu' as activation function, and the last one use softmax to give the probabilities of the outputs. Before the fully-connected dense layers for classification, the networks perform a channel concatenation process.

5 Experiments

This section presents the details of the experimental setup and applied datasets for the evaluation of the proposed system for vehicle recognition as follows:

5.1 Experimental Setup

The proposed system was designed and tested on high-performance machines to reduce the training and testing time. NVIDIA Quadro p6000 was used, having 3840 CUDA cores and an 8 GB memory. In these experiments, Linux Ubuntu 18.04 LTS operating system was used with Cuda 10.2, cuDNN v7.5.0, Python 3.6 with its deep learning libraries such as Keras, TensorFlow etc.

5.2 Datasets

We have used different datasets for experiments as shown in Table 2. Stanford Cars-196 dataset contains a total of 16185 images of cars having 196 classes with almost 50 by 50 division among training and testing data. The training part of the dataset contains 8144 images in 196 classes of cars and the testing part of the dataset contains 8041 images in 196 classes of cars. The VMMR dataset is much larger in scale and diversity compared with the existing car image datasets. The VMMRdb dataset has 9,170 classes that cover the vehicle models from 1950 to 2016. However, the distribution in different classes of the dataset is highly imbalanced (i.e. some classes contain thousands of images while others contain only 35 images). Therefore, we have used a subset of this dataset VMMR-51 which contains 51 classes with 1986 training samples and 1984 testing samples but experiments in this paper are only performed on the Stanford Cars196 dataset. The dataset for color recognition consists of 15601 total number of images divided into 8 different vehicle colors. To simplify, we have only used five classes for vehicle color recognition.

Table 2. Datasets used for training and testing

Stanford Car dataset [20]	161 classes of 196 vehicle models for vehicle make	16185 images and model recognition
Vehicle make and model Recognition [19]	291752 images but 9170 classes for vehicle highly imbalanced	Make & model recognition dataset
Vehicle color recognition [10]	Images of 8 different vehicle colors	15601 images
License plate dataset Open ALPR + local LPs		1300 images

6 Evaluation and Results: Benchmark Methods

We extensively evaluated the performance of different CNN architectures and compared them to state-of-the-art methods on vehicle make and model recognition as shown in graph 1. For ALPR, we have used Sergio's work as a benchmark where the author used Warped Planar Object Detection Network (WPOD NET) which was trained on AOLP dataset to detect the license plate of the extracted vehicle. The final step was to read the License plate of the extracted vehicle which was done by using OCR Network with 93.29% accuracy while misclassifying a few characters as shown in Fig. 2. Therefore, we have implemented another approach as discussed in Sect. 4.2 which is more accurate by successfully recognizing all characters on the license plate. In order to recognize the color of the vehicle, we have first implemented the k-nearest neighbor trained on five major colors i.e. black, white, red, blue, and yellow according to their respective RBG values. Later, a novel deep neural network for vehicle color recognition has been proposed in this paper which is more accurate and computationally inexpensive for this task. The CNN architecture used in [18] Reza's model for vehicle color recognition which consists of 16 layers is used as an evaluation for vehicle color recognition. The proposed model was also trained and tested on the same vehicle color dataset [10] which we have used for our model. We have increased the depth of the neural network up to 21 layers and before feed up to fully-connected layers, the networks do a channel concatenation process. This has resulted in overall improved accuracy by 1.2%. License Plate Detection and Recognition using Warped Planar Object Detection Network (Wpod-Net) has been used, which is trained on AOLP dataset to detect the license plate of the extracted vehicle.

Table 3. Summary of experimental results

Module	Model	Training Accuracy	Testing Accuracy
Vehicle Detection	Yolo V3 [3]	98.88%	98.32%
Make & Model	ResNet-152 [25]	92.0%	81.37%
Make & Model	Xception [22]	97.8%	96.45%
Colour Recognition	CNN	97.4%	88.9%

The next step is to read the License plate of the extracted vehicle which is done by using OCR Network. Although, this method was useful in recognizing distorted license plates with higher accuracy but misclassifying a few characters. Therefore, we adopted another approach that is more accurate and easier to integrate with other modules of this system with higher output accuracy. For vehicle make and model recognition, we have found that Xception has outperformed other state-of-the-art deep learning architectures as shown in Table 1. Since the images contain large background areas, we used the annotation of bounding boxes for both testing and training using the Stanford dataset. To increase the accuracy of these models, we have performed augmentation on the dataset in the form of rotation, scaling, and lighting. Stanford Car dataset was trained with the split of 50% for training and 50% for testing. The hyper-perimeters for training were 100 epochs, with a batch size of 32, and a learning rate of 0.001. This resulted in improved accuracy of 92% accuracy using ResNet-152. The summary of obtained results is shown in Table 3. We also implemented different most promising CNNs architectures for image classification and xception has been found to improve the achieved accuracy with 13% on testing dataset and outperformed other state-of-the-art models such as DenseNet-161 and ResNet152 as shown in Table 1. Xception not only outperformed other stateof-the-art CNNs for image classification but also among the models with fewer parameters as shown in Fig. 4.

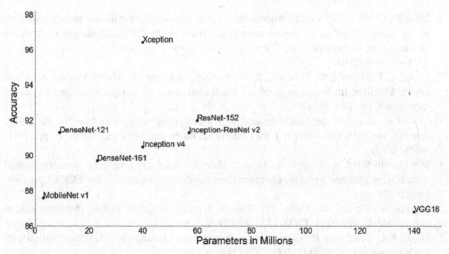

Fig. 4. Accuracy of different deep learning models in reference to their number of parameters

7 Conclusion

This paper has integrated ALPR with vehicle color, make and model recognition to identify the stolen vehicles. The system performs pre-processing operations and uses YOLOv3 to extract the vehicle from the scene. Then WPOD-NET is implemented on the detected area of the vehicle for detecting and rectifying distorted license plate in an image. Later, an OCR is employed for character recognition of the license plate number. Besides, another more efficient method for ALPR has also been discussed in this paper. The system also identifies other attributes of the vehicle such as vehicle color, make and model. The make and model recognition is performed via deep learning using Xception which is trained on the Stanford Cars-196 dataset while different state-of-the-art models have also been investigated for comparison using the same dataset. The color recognition was first carried out using K-Nearest Neighbors (KNN) Machine Learning Classifier which is trained on R, G, B Color values. However, a novel deep neural network for vehicle color recognition has been proposed in this paper which is more accurate and computationally inexpensive for this task. Finally, these extracted features are matched with the vehicle license plate, while performing the stolen license plate checking using a centralized database. When a vehicle fails the verification process or attribute matching with the license plate process, it will be deemed as stolen or illegal.

Acknowledgement. This research work was funded by the Higher Education Commission (HEC) Pakistan and Ministry of Planning Development and Reforms under the National Center in Big Data and Cloud Computing.

References

1. MacCarthy, J.: Vehicle surveillance and control system. U.S. Patent7,548,803, issued 16 June 2009

2. Dhar, P., Guha, S., Biswas, T., Abedin, M.Z.: A system design for license plate recognition by using edge detection and convolution neural network. In: 2018 International Conference on Computer, Communication, Chemical, Material and Electronic Engineering (IC4ME2), pp. 1–4. IEEE (2018)
3. Redmon, J., Divvala, S., Girshick, R., Farhadi, A.: You only lookonce: Unified, real-time object detection. In: Proceedings of the IEEE conference on computer vision and pattern recognition, pp. 779–788 (2016)
4. Laroca, R., et al.: A robust realtime automatic license plate recognition based on the YOLO detector. In: 2018 International Joint Conference on Neural Networks (IJCNN), pp. 1–10. IEEE (2018)
5. Montazzolli Silva, S., Jung, C.R.: License plate detection andrecognition in unconstrained scenarios. In: Proceedings of the European Conference on Computer Vision (ECCV), pp. 580–596 (2018)
6. Shapiro, V., Georgi, G., Dimo, D.: Towards a multinationalcar license plate recognition system. Mach. Vis. Appl. **17**(3), 173–183 (2006)
7. Deole, P.A., Longadge, R.: Content based image retrieval usingcolor feature extraction with KNN classification. IJCSMC **3**(5), 12741280 (2014)
8. Zhang, M., Wang, P., Zhang, X.: Vehicle color recognitionusing deep convolutional neural networks. In: Proceedings of the 2019 International Conference on Artificial Intelligence and Computer Science, pp. 236–238 (2019)
9. Zhang, Q., Zhuo, L., Li, J., Zhang, J., Zhang, H., Li, X.: Vehicle color recognition using multiple-layer feature representations of lightweight convolutional neural network. Signal Process. **147**, 146–153 (2018)
10. Chen, P., Bai, X., Liu, W.: Vehicle color recognition on urban roadby feature context. IEEE Trans. Intell. Transp. Syst. **15**(5), 2340–2346 (2014)
11. Hongliang, B., Changping, L.: A hybrid license plate extraction methodbased on edge statistics and morphology. In: Proceedings of the 17th International Conference on Pattern Recognition, 2004. ICPR 2004, vol. 2, pp. 831–834. IEEE (2004)
12. Anagnospoulos, C.-N.E.: License plate recognition: A brief turial. IEEE Intelligent transportation systems magazine **6**(1), 59–67 (2014)
13. Anagnospoulos, C.-N., Anagnospoulos, I.E., Psoroulas, I.D., Loumos, V., Kayafas, E.: License plate recognition from still images and video sequences: A survey. IEEE Trans. Intell. Transp. Syst. **9**(3), 377–391 (2008)
14. Yang, L., Luo, P., Loy, C.C., Tang, X.: A large-scale cardataset for fine-grained categorization and verification. In: Proceedings of the IEEE conference on computer vision and pattern recognition, pp. 3973–3981 (2015)
15. Xie, L., Ahmad, T., Jin, L., Liu, Y., Zhang, S.: A newCNN-based method for multi-directional car license plate detection. IEEE Trans. Intell. Transp. Syst. **19**(2), 507–517 (2018)
16. Al-Shemarry, M.S., Li, Y., Abdulla, S.: Ensemble of adaboostcascades of 3L-LBPs classifiers for license plates detection with low quality images. Expert Systems with Applications **92**, 216–235 (2018)
17. Laroca, R., et al.: A robust real-time aumatic license plate recognition based on the YOLO detecr. In: 2018 International Joint Conference on Neural Networks (IJCNN), pp. 1–10. IEEE (2018)
18. Rachmadi, R.F., Purnama, I.: Vehicle color recognition using convolutional neural network. arXiv preprint arXiv:1510.07391 (2015)
19. Tafazzoli, F., Frigui, H., Nishiyama, K.: A large and diversedataset for improved vehicle make and model recognition. In: Proceedings of the IEEE Conference on Computer Vision and Pattern Recognition Workshops, pp. 1–8 (2017)

20. Krause, J., Stark, M., Deng, J., Fei-Fei, L.: 3d object representations for fine-grained categorization. In: Proceedings of the IEEE international conference on computer vision workshops,
pp. 554–561 (2013)

21. Jung, H., Choi, M.-K., Jung, J., Lee, J.-H., Kwon, S., Jung, W.Y.: ResNet-based vehicle
classification and localization in traffic surveillance systems. In: Proceedings of the IEEE
conference on computer vision and pattern recognition workshops, pp. 61–67 (2017)

22. Chollet, F.: Xception: deep learning with depthwise separable convolutions. In: 2017 IEEE
Conference on Computer Vision and Pattern Recognition (CVPR), Honolulu, HI, pp. 1800–
1807 (2017). https://doi.org/10.1109/CVPR.2017.195

23. Szegedy, C., Ioffe, S., Vanhoucke, V., Alemi, A.A.: Inception-v4, inception-ResNet and
the impact of residual connections on learning. In: Proceedings of the Thirty-First AAAI
Conference on Artificial Intelligence (AAAI'17). AAAI Press, pp. 4278–4284 (2017)

24. Liu, S., Deng, W.: Very deep convolutional neural network based imageclassification using
small training sample size. In: 2015 3rd IAPR Asian Conference on Pattern Recognition
(ACPR), Kuala Lumpur, pp. 730–734 (2015). https://doi.org/10.1109/ACPR.2015.7486599

25. Huang, G., Liu, Z., van der Maaten, L., Weinberger, K.Q.: Densely connectedconvolu-
tional networks. In: Proceedings of the IEEE Conference on Computer Vision and Pattern
Recognition (2017)

26. Howard, A.G., et al.: Mobilenets: efficient convolutional neural networks for mobile vision
applications. arXiv preprint arXiv:1704.04861 (2017)

27. He, K., Zhang, X., Ren, S., Sun, J.: Deep residual learning for image recognition. arXiv
preprint arXiv:1512.03385 (2015)

IMMFV2: Improved Modified Fermat Factorization Algorithm

Fahed Ali[1]([⊠]) and Mehwish Mustafa[2]

[1] Department of Computer Science, The Islamia University of Bahawalpur, Bahawalpur, Pakistan
fhdpgc@yahoo.com
[2] Department of Information Technology, University of Gujarat, Gujarat, Pakistan

Abstract. Network security has intense significance and worth in the protection of the system from unauthorized access or threats. Denial of service, illicit access, executing commands illegally, confidentiality violation and breaching, data diddling and destruction of data are the main threats which a network may have to cope up with. Numerous techniques and algorithms are extensively implemented and manipulated in order to enhance the security and safety of networks and to make it unbreakable and inaccessible to unauthorized and unofficial access and attacks. Cryptography has its own importance in network security. RSA is the public key cryptosystem. The RSA algorithm is most extensively used in network security. In this paper there is comparison and analysis of RSA factoring Algorithms with our proposed technique. We will analyze and evaluate the performance of different Fermat Factoring Algorithms which are Modified Fermat Factorization and Modified Fermat Factorization V2 and its comparison with our proposed Improved modified Fermat Factorization V2. The calculations have been given in detail and these calculations have been calculated and evaluated in net beans software. And the comparison will be demonstrated in experimental results. The comparison after calculation will show that IMMFV2 is better in implementation as compared to MFF and MFFV2.

Keywords: RSA Scheme · Modified fermat factorization · Modified fermat factorization version 2 · Improved modified fermat factorization V2 · Possible Prime Modified Fermat Factorization

1 Introduction

Cryptography is fundamentally a method or technique to ensure the security of data by applying encryption and decryption to the data to be communicated [18]. Secure communication is its purpose even in the presence of adversaries. And cryptosystem is basically that suite or pair of algorithms which work under the technique of Cryptography. According to the method of cryptography, while communicating data through network, the data should only be understandable to the receiver and sender. Sender sends plain text and then it gets encrypted and converted into cipher text. Why we convert the Plain text into cipher text by using any technique? It is because we desire to secure it

© Springer Nature Switzerland AG 2022
D. N. A. Jawawi et al. (Eds.): ESMoC 2021, CCIS 1615, pp. 114–122, 2022.
https://doi.org/10.1007/978-3-031-19968-4_12

from unauthorized access. When it reaches the receiver end, it gets decrypted and again transform into plain text. The design and analysis of today's cryptographic algorithms are exceptionally mathematical. There are two keys use in cryptosystem: 1) Private Key Cryptosystem 2) Public Key Cryptosystem. The concept of the public key cryptosystem was proposed by Diffie and Hellman [5] in 1976. Since then, a number of public-key cryptosystems have been proposed to realize the notion of public-key cryptosystems. Authenticity, confidentiality, and protection of authenticity of public keys are the prime advantages of public key Cryptosystem [19]. In private key cryptosystem, there is key cryptosystem that for data decryption the encryption can be processed with the secret or private key is must.

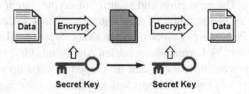

Fig. 1. Public key cryptography

Always have one key for encryption and decryption [1]. Private Key is also known as symmetric key. In public key cryptosystem, two keys have been introduced, one is private key and other is public key [1]. Figure 1 will bring into view the method of public key cryptography. The Fig. 1 is explaining the concept of public There are many methods used in public key cryptography such as PGP, GPG, S/MIME, etc.

Transport Layer Security, Digital Signature (DSA), Diffie Hellman, RSA and ElGamal are names of some of public key cryptography methods and algorithms. The RSA Cryptography algorithm is a public key cryptography algorithm and it was initially originated in 1977 by Ron Rivest, Adi Shamir and Leonard Adelman [1]. The purpose to create such algorithm was to assure security of data from unknown and unspecified persons and illicit access. The RSA algorithm is predominantly in use in order to enhance the security of the data at both sender and receiver end [12]. The basic function of RSA is to enhance the security of data or information between sender and receiver [13].

Select e, e is relatively prime to $\varphi(n)$ and less than $\varphi(n)$. Conclude d, de $= 1$ (mod $\varphi(n)$) and d $< \varphi(n)$.

Transport Layer Security, Digital Signature (DSA), Diffie Hellman, RSA and ElGamal are names of some of public key cryptography methods and algorithms. The RSA Cryptography algorithm is a public key cryptography algorithm and it was initially originated in 1977 by Ron Rivest, Adi Shamir and Leonard Adelman [1]. The purpose to create such algorithm was to assure security of data from unknown and unspecified persons and illicit access. The RSA algorithm is predominantly in use in order to enhance the security of the data at both sender and receiver end [12]. The basic function of RSA is to enhance the security of data or information between sender and receiver [13]. Below is given the RSA cryptography Algorithm:

RSA Algorithm: The steps of RSA Algorithm are:

Select two prime numbers, p and q.

Find n, n = p*q.

Find $\varphi(n) = (p-1)(q-1)$.

Basically, we need two prime numbers for generating an RSA key pair. Because it is always easy to multiply any two prime numbers but is complex and difficult to reverse it into two prime factors again. If you are capable of factoring the public key and find these prime numbers, you will then be able to find the private key. The whole security of RSA is based on the fact that it is not easy to factorize large composite numbers, that's why the length of the key highly changes the robustness of the RSA algorithm. The strength of RSA basically depends upon the complexity of factoring a very large number. The protection and security of cryptosystem of the RSA is built upon the procedure of factorization of great integers. This is called RSA problem. In Cryptosystem, The Pollard's p-1 algorithm, Quadratic Sieve, Trial Division algorithm, Vfactor [4], MV Factor [5], Fermat Factorization Algorithm (FF) [3], MFF [3], MFFV2 [5] and MFFV3 [6], were introduced and developed to cope up with RSA factoring problem. The purpose of these algorithms was to minimize the computational time and few of the algorithms were developed to decrease even the computational iterations. The first factoring algorithm was Fermat Improved version of FF. The purpose of MFF was to improve the computational time. The MFFV2 was the improved version of MFF. This algorithm was modification in the previous Fermat factorization algorithm MFF.

We proposed a new method in this paper which is Improved Modified Fermat Factorization V2 (IMFFV2). In IMFFV2, we will decrease the computational time and computational iterations by using hexadecimal numbers. Because, In hexadecimal, during computation, the least significant digits 2, 3, 5, 6, 7, 8, A, B, C, D, E and F, these numbers not computed so we use this technique and try to decrease the more computational time and computational iterations. We will proof that our method is more suitable as compared to other factoring algorithms. Factorization (FF). Fermat factorization Algorithm deals with the difference of two negative variable values and determine the odd integer to which in factoring Algorithms we consider as N. FF was created to resolve the RSA factoring Algorithm which was later modified and known as modified Fermat factorization Algorithm (MFF).

2   Literature Review

Many factorization Algorithms has been developed to cope up with RSA factoring problem [6]. These algorithms tried to enhance the performance by decreasing the computational time and by decreasing computational iterations.

2.1   General Purpose Algorithm

The general purpose algorithms can be functional to factorize the digits of any form. The running time of these algorithms depends on the size of the digits to factorize. There are many general purpose algorithms which are Quadratic Sieve (QS) [8], Multi Polynomial Quadratic Sieve (MPQS) [8], Continued Fraction (CFRAC) [9], factor base and General Number Field Sieve (GNFS) [10]. These factoring algorithms use the similar technique.

Fermat Factorization algorithm (FF): Pierre de Fermat worked on developing a new method which was Fermat Factorization algorithm in 1600 [3]. There Are two integers used in the Fermat Factorization algorithms are x and y and the n is equal to $x^2 - y^2$ ($n = x^2 - y^2$). Where x and y are (p + q)/2 and (p − q)/2 respectively. The p and q are prime numbers.

Modified Fermat Factorization (MFF): The modified version of the Fermat Factorization is Modified Fermat Factorization (MFF) [3]. In MFF method more improve the factorization time of n and decreases the factorization time of n. So the new equation of y is $y = \sqrt{(x^2 - n)}$. In first step we getting the value of x from the square root of the n and use the ceil function to get the value of x. the equation of x is $x = ceil \sqrt{n}$. Now find the y from the new equation, if they are not an integer so adding 1 in x, the x = x + 1, now computing and find the value of y but the value of y is must be an integer, stop the processing when y is an integer. After finding the x and y, then find the values of p and q which the equation of p = x + y and q = x − y, which are two prime numbers of n.

Modified Fermat Factorization Version 2 (MFFV2): The modified version of Modified Fermat Factorization is Modified Fermat Factorization version 2 (MFFV2) [5]. This method is more improve the previous version which was Modified Fermat Factorization. More decrease the computing time of Modified Fermat Factorization. If the least significant numbers are 2, 3, 7, or 8 than it not computing the square root of its computes If LSD are 0, 1, 4, 5, 6 and 9 than it is square root of y. due to decreasing the iterations, if the least significant numbers are 2, 3, 7 or 8, so the consuming time is very less.

Possible Prime Modified Fermat Factorization: P2MFF was modified from MFF and MFFV. For P2MFF the authors didn't choose all the values of x which is in range of sqrt (n) to n to find the integer y, because some values of x are not in the form: n = 6k−1 or n = 6k + 1. P2mff can reduce computational time as compared to MFF. It can increase speed by applying two concepts: one is reducing no. of times to compute the square root of integer when its least significant digit is 2,3,7,8 the method is used in MFFV2, the other is from the number theory that if an integer is a perfect square, the result of this integer modulo 4 must be only 0 or 1. The algorithm of p2mff is distinguished in two cases: n = 6k−1 and n = 6k + 1.

2.2 Pollard P Method

Monte Carlo proposed a method in 1975. The proposed method was pollard technique. Pollard technique was the distinct purpose method [15]. The main purpose of the pollard method is to factorize the large numbers. It finds the p, due to the recurrence of the module.

3 The Proposed Method: IMFFV Algorithm

We proposed a new method of factoring algorithm which is Improved Modified Fermat Factorization V2 (IMFFV2) Algorithm. The Modified Fermat Factorization method checks all the numbers but in MFFV2, if the least significant digits of y2 are 2, 3, 7 or 8 then it's not computed. In IMFFV2, the computational iterations are reduced and the computational time is reduced as compared to MFFV2. In IMFFV2, we will use hexadecimal technique. In this technique just 0, 1, 4 and 9 numbers computed and other remains un computed because 0, 1, 4 and 9 numbers least significant digits. In IMFFV2, if the least significant digits of y2 are 0, 1, 4 or 9 then it will be compute. We will compute just four digits and will not compute twelve digits. As a result of which it will be increasing the computational speed but decreasing the computational time. If the computational time decreases than there should be decrease in number of iterations.

3.1 Algorithm: IMMFV2

1. n = semiprime number
2. $x = \text{ceil} (\sqrt{n})$
3. $y^2 = (x^2 - n)$.
4. If lsd of y^2 is 0, 1, 4 or 9, then go to step 5 else go to step 6.
5. y is a perfect square, then go to step 7 else go to step 6.
6. $x = x + 1$ and go to step 3.
7. $p = x + y$ and $q = x - y$ are two factors of n.

In Table 1, we have selected some prime numbers to apply IMMFV2 algorithm technique. The prime numbers are secure to use because they are difficult to reverse.

Table 1. Prime numbers

1009	1019	1021	1031	1033	1039	1049	1051	1061	1063
1069	1087	1091	1093	1097	1103	1109	1117	1123	1129
1151	1153	1163	1171	1181	1187	1193	1201	1213	1217
1229	1231	1237	1249	1259	1277	1279	1283	1289	1291
1297	1301	1303	1307	1319	1321	1327	1361	1367	1373
1381	1399	1409	1423	1427	1429	1433	1439	1447	1451
1453	1459	1471	1481	1483	1487	1489	1493	1499	1511
1523	1531	1543	1549	1553	1559	1567	1571	1579	1583
1597	1601	1607	1609	1613	1619	1627	1637	1657	1663
1667	1669	1693	1699	1709	1721	1723	1733	1741	1747
1759	1777	1783	1787	1789	1801	1811	1831	1847	1861
1867	1871	1873	1877	1879	1889	1901	1907	1913	1931
1933	1949	1951	1973	1979	1987	1993	1997	1999	2003

As discussed earlier that we multiply two prime numbers to get semi prime numbers because these are difficult to reverse. In Table 2 the list of semi prime numbers (multiplication of two prime numbers) is given.

Table 2. Semi prime numbers

1003	1007	1027	1055	1067	1081	1111	1121	1133	1157
1167	1177	1199	1211	1227	1261	1285	1313	1343	1369
1387	1391	1393	1417	1465	1477	1501	1537	1681	1687
1689	1727	1751	1781	1807	1849	1873	1909	1919	1937

Table 3. Hexadecimal square numbers

Number	Square	Number	Square	Number	Square
32	9C4	64	2710	96	57E4
33	A29	65	27B9	97	5911
34	A90	66	28A4	98	5A40
35	AF9	67	2971	99	5B71
36	B64	68	2A40	100	10000
37	BD1	69	2B11	101	10201
38	C40	70	3100	102	10404
39	CB1	71	31E1	103	10609
40	1000	72	32C4	104	10810
41	1081	73	33A9	105	10A19
42	1104	74	3490	106	10C24
43	1189	75	3579	107	10E31
44	1210	76	3664	108	11040
45	1299	77	3751	109	11251
46	1324	78	3840	110	12100
47	13B1	79	3931	111	12321

Table 3; illustrate the hexadecimal numbers with their squares. We have used hexadecimal numbers in IMMFV2. The hexadecimal numbers are 0–9 and then use the letters A–F.

4 Experimental Results

The experimental results demonstrate the comparisons between MFF, MFFV2 and IMFFV2. The results are divided in two parts. First part is related with computational time and second part related with computational iterations. Table 4; show the results of computational time between MFF, MFFV2 and IMFFV2. The results show that, the IMFFV2 is taking less computational time for factorization rather than MFF and MFFV2. Due to less computational time, the speed is fast and reduces the iterations. Table 5 shows the comparison of the results of computational iterations between MFF, MFFV2 and IMFFV2. Both results show that the IMFFV2 algorithm is very fast and accurate algorithm for factoring the semi prime numbers. The Big Integer Class in Java is chosen to implement these factoring algorithms MFF, MFFV2 and IMFFV2. The big Integer Class in java takes the infinite numbers. The table below shows, comparison results between MFF, MFFV2 and IMFFV2.

In Table 4, the computational time between MFF, MFFV2 and IMFFV2 are displayed. The results show that the performance of IMFFV2 is better as compared to MFF and

Table 4. Computational time

n = p * q	Computing y2 (Computational Time)		
	MFF	MFFV2	IMFFV2
34148097482646341 = 193950553 x 176065997	0.65	0.50	0.06
28141005701727301 = 207752947 x 135454183	10.49	7.58	1.57
5883255032751007097 = 2622941411x 2242999027	20.45	11.47	3.36
337838988533956487317 = 18949526263x17828360659	24.94	13.52	4.25

MFFV2 because IMFFV2 takes less time in contrast with MFF and MFFV2 in all cases. In 34148097482646341, MFF takes 0.65 s and MFFV2 takes 0.50 s but IMFFV2 takes just 0.06 s. SoIMFFV2 is better than MFF and MFFV2.

In Fig. 2, the computational time between MFF, MFFV2 and IMFFV2 are shown. The results show that IMFFV2 produces better results than MFF and MFFV2 because IMFFV2 takes less time than the time taken by MFF and MFFV2 in all cases. In 34148097482646341, MFF takes 0.65 s and MFFV2 takes 0.50 s but IMFFV2 takes just 0.06 s. So IMFFV2 is better than MFF and MFFV2.

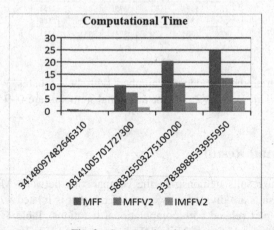

Fig. 2. Computational time

Table 5, the computational iterations between MFF, MFFV2 and IMFFV2 are displayed. The results show that IMFFV2 is better than MFF and MFFV2 because IMFFV2 has taken less computational iterations when compared with MFF and MFFV2 in all cases. In 34148097482646341, MFF takes 216237 iterations and MFFV2 takes 129743 iterations but IMFFV2 takes just 54058 iterations. So IMFFV2 is better than MFF and MFFV2.

In Fig. 3, the computational iterations between MFF, MFFV2 and IMFFV2 are shown. The results show that IMFFV2 is better than MFF and MFFV2 because IMFFV2

Table 5. Computational Iterations

n = p * q	Computing y2 (Computational Iterations)		
	MFF	MFFV2	IMFFV2
34148097482646341 = 193950553 x 176065997	216237	129743	54058
28141005701727301 = 207752947 x135454183	3850754	2310453	962688
5883255032751007097 = 2622941411 x 2242999027	7428005	2971203	1857000
337838988533956487317 = 18949526263x17828360659	8546607	3418644	2136651

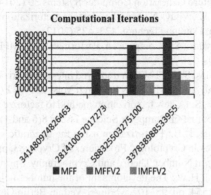

Fig. 3. Computational Iterations

has taken less computational iterations when compared to MFF and MFFV2 in all cases. In 3.41481E + 16, MFF takes 216237 iterations and MFFV2 takes 129743 iterations but IMFFV2 takes just 54058 iterations. So IMFFV2 is better than MFF and MFFV2.

5 Conclusion

Managing the computational time in every Algorithm is very important. This improved modified Fermat Factorization V2 (IMFFV2) algorithm is more effective and efficient, as it requires lesser computational time and the number of iterations are also reduced significantly. The purpose of IMFFV2 essentially is to improve performance of system by providing better results by reduction in the computational time. It is evident from the results that our approach provides better performance by significantly improving the results. The experimental results show that IMFFV2 is more suitable for other factoring algorithms. The results also show that IMFFV2, find the elements of n much faster than MFF and MFFV2. In future we can work further on enhancing the capability of IMFFV2 algorithm. The more improvement in this IMFFV2 is to reduce the more computational time. If reducing the more computational time, then must be reducing the iterations then the speed will be increase which is basically the purpose of this RSA algorithm.

References

1. Somsuk, K.: The new integer factorization algorithm based on Fermat's factorization algorithm and Euler's theorem **10**(2), 1469-1476 (April 2020)
2. Bahig, H.M., Bahig, H.M., Kotb, Y.: Fermat factorization using a multi-core system. Int. J. Adva. Comp. Sci. Appli. **11**(4) (2020)
3. Somsuk, K., Tientanopajai, K.: An Improvement of Fermat's Factorization by Considering the Last m Digits of Modulus to Decrease Computation Time **19**(1), 99–111 (2017 Jan.)
4. Ambedkar, B.R., Gupta, A., Gautam, P., Bedi, S.S.: An efficient method to factorize the RSA public key encryption. In: Proceeding of International Conference on Communication Systems and Network Technologies, pp. 108–111 (2011)
5. Wu, M.-E., Tso, R., Sun, H.-M.: On the improvement of Fermat factorization using a continued fraction technique. Future Generation Computer Systems 30 (2014)
6. Sharma, P., Gupta, A.K., Vijay, A.: Modified integer factorization algorithm using V-Factor method. Adva. Comp. Commu. Technol. 423–425 (2012)
7. Somsuk, K., Kasemvilas, S.: Comparison Performance of MFFV2 and MV Factor for Factoring the Modulus
8. Somsuk, K., Kasemvilas, S.: MFFV3: an improved integer factorization algorithm to increase computation speed. Advanced Materials Research Vols. 931–932 (2014)
9. Ambedkar, B.R., Bedi, S.: A new factorization method to factorize rsa public key encryption. IJCSI International Journal of Computer Science Issues **8**(6 and 1), (2011 November)
10. Davis, J.A., Hold ridge, D.B.: Factorization using the quadratic sieve algorithm. In: David Chaum, (ed.) Advances in Cryptology: Procedures of Crypto 83, pp. 103–113. Plenum Press
11. Koblitz, N.: A Course in Number Theory and Cryptography. Springer-Verlag, New York
12. Lenstra, A.K., Lenstra, H.W.: The development of the number field sieve. In: Lecture Notes in Mathematics, vol 1554, pp. 95–102. Springer-Verlag, Berlin Germany
13. Kwon, T.-W., You, C.-S., Heo, W.-S., Kang, Y.-K., Choi, J.-R.: Two implementation methods of a 1024-bit RSA crypto processor based on modified Montgomery algorithm. Circuits and Systems, 2001. ISCAS 2001, pp. 650–653 (2001)
14. Hwang, R.-J., Feng-Fu, S.: An Efficient Decryption Method for RSA Cryptosystem, Advanced Information Networking and Applications. AINA **2005**, 585–590 (2005)
15. Vignesh, R.S., Sudharssum, S., Kumar, K.J.J.: Limitations of quantum & the versatility of classical cryptography: a comparative study. Environmental and Computer Science, 2009. ICECS '09, pp. 333-337 (2009). http://en.wikipedia.org/wiki/Square_number
16. Tao, J., Ma, J., Keranen, M., Mayo, J.: RSA visual: A Visualization Tool for the RSA Cipher
17. Usman, M., Bajwa, Z., Afzal, M.: New factoring algorithm: prime factoring algorithm. IJMER **5**(1), 75–77 (2015 February)
18. Kessler, G.C.: An Overview of Cryptography (7 July 2016)

Software Quality

Functional Requirements Management in Virtual Team Environment

Zara Mansoor[1]([✉]), Salman Qadri[2], and Sunnia Ikram[1]

[1] Department of Software Engineering, The Islamia University of Bahawalpur, Bahawalpur, Pakistan
zaramansoor36@gmail.com
[2] Deptartment of Computer Science, MNS University of Agriculture, Multan, Pakistan
rafaqat.kazmi@iub.edu.pk

Abstract. Software Requirements play an important role in the Software development environment. Functional requirements capture and specify specific intended behavior of the system being developed, so well managed requirements help for the further design, development and deployment aspects. Functional requirements management is playing a vital role in a virtual team environment. Functional Requirements Specification documents the operations and activities that a system must be able to perform so in a virtual team environment it looks very difficult to manage the task of functional requirements of any system. This research focuses on the well manage requirement framework in a virtual team environment.

Keywords: Requirement management · Virtual environment · Functional requirements · Non-functional requirements

1 Introduction

Word "Virtual" means being in an influence or essence, but not in fact. So, by virtual environment we mean the environment which is not physically present in real, but it is created by a system or software to appear. A virtual environment is an environment or organization in which people are working interdependently with a shared purpose across time, space and organizational boundaries using technologies. Due to communication technology improvements and continued globalization, virtual teams have increased rapidly worldwide. [10]. The area of the virtual environment under our discussion is "The functional requirement management in a virtual team environment". We all know that Software Requirements play an important role in the Software development environment. Requirement management is a process to manage the entire user requirements of software or a system. The most crucial of all requirements is the functional requirement of the system. The intended behavior of the system is term as its functional requirement. Functional requirements management is playing a vital role in a virtual team environment. Functional Requirements Specification documents the operations and activities that a system must be able to perform, so in a virtual team environment it looks very difficult to manage the task of functional requirements of any system. Nowadays companies

D. N. A. Jawawi et al. (Eds.): ESMoC 2021, CCIS 1615, pp. 125–133, 2022.
https://doi.org/10.1007/978-3-031-19968-4_13

are heavily investing in virtual teams to enhance their performance and competitiveness [12].

This research focuses the well manage requirement framework in a virtual team environment. Although the virtual environment is a leading business trend still it is facing numerous issues or problems. Lack of communication is one of the most prominent and vital issue. The main issue under our discussion is that "how should we work in a virtual team environment to optimize the management of the functional requirements of a system?" Since the intended behavior of system is term as its functional requirement. So, we can say that functional requirement is of core importance and if we optimize the management of functional requirements, it will make the overall management of system more efficient.

To conduct our research, we have gone through the work which had been done previously in the domain of the virtual environment and functional requirements. As well as the tools or engines which were being developed. [13] Summary of the work done by various scholars or researchers in given below: Ye Li et al. had suggested a theoretical model based on extended adaptive structuration theory (EAST). The result suggested that behavioral cultural intelligence and language proficiency is crucial in cross-cultural communication and peer trust. Therefore, while recruiting a team member in cross-cultural environment their language proficiency and cultural intelligence must be kept in mind along with their technical skills [1].

2 Literature Review

Virtual research environment is an evolving concept which tends to address the difficult challenges related to guiding collaborative research. Kaushal et al. had reported research to investigate how the collaborative research's success factors can be attained by organizing and arranging the virtual research environment [2]. Anne Powell et al. had reviewed some previous work and literature related to virtual teams to provide a firm understanding of virtual teams and their current state of work. By reviewing various aspects of virtual teams like inputs, socio-emotional processes, task processes and outputs they have developed various research questions which would be helpful in carrying out future research as well as in lying practical formation of effective virtual teams [3]. Bavota et al. presented an integrated and practical Methodology to teach Software Engineering (SE) and Software Project Management (SPM) courses [14]. Thamhain reported the result of a recent field study examining the situations helping collaboration in various development companies. The author had described various organizational conditions, leadership challenges, managerial actions, and work processes that can be improved or customized to develop ease of communication among team members so that best results can be achieved [4]. Lai and Ali, 2013 had gone through previous methods by which requirement management is done or handled. They had concluded that the requirement management method used for collocated software development projects cannot be used effectively for global software development projects. So, they had presented a requirement management method to deal with this issue. They had validated the method by implementing it in a controlled laboratory environment using a case study for an online shopping system. [5], Uma Viswanath, 2014 has described how it will help the organization to meet the challenges by allowing some authorized team to take the right decision for the project [16]. Linda Westfall, 2006 had described the various levels and types of requirements. She said that to get desired software the requirements should be specified correctly and timely. A detailed view is given by her including WHAT: are various requirement, WHY: they are described, WHO: describes them, WHEN: are they define and HOW: techniques are used to specify, verify, analyze and validate software requirements [6]. Dhirendra Pandey and U. Suman, 2010 have suggested the importance of requirement engineering. They have stated requirement engineering as the initial and most crucial part of the software engineering process. They have proposed an effective requirement engineering process model for software development. In order to produce good quality software [7], this is an era of E economy, so the process of management is going through major changes in each dimension of basic management function. New results in communication problems are constantly reshaping the management process. Vlado Dimovski and Sandra Penger, 2002 have explained how new economy has influenced the fundamental functions of the management process in any new era organization. [9]. V. Sadana and X.F. Liu, 2007 have presented the framework for the detection of conflict among non-functional requirement by using the joined examination of functional and non-functional requirement [15]. Nelly Manevahad described her personal experience gained during one of her outsourcing project. She had also mentioned few possible directions for future research [13].

After going through various research papers on virtual team and functional requirements we have reached to a conclusion that none of them have suggested that if we optimize the management of functional requirements in virtual team environment the whole management and development process will become more efficient.

By conducting an intensive study about requirements management, it was noticed that the requirement management method used for collocated software development projects cannot be used effectively for global software development projects [5]. Hence, a different methodology is required to manage functional requirements in virtual team environment. Requirement engineering is the initial and most crucial part of software engineering process [7], hence if we optimize the management of requirements, specifically functional requirements it will make the overall management of the system more efficient.

Virtual team has no hierarchy, which means there is no common hierarchical structure among the virtual team [3], however, Powell, Piccoli and Ives have found and studied 43 articles on virtual teams and established that the existing investigation has found four key center zones of it.

3   Proposed Methodology

According to our proposed framework first when the leader has prioritized the requirement already, considering the first requirement, we will differentiate it into functional and non-functional requirements if it's a functional requirement then is a priority will be judged that either it's the highest priority requirement or not. If it's the highest priority requirement then the system will accept it and it will be executed otherwise, we will go back and check for the highest priority requirement again.

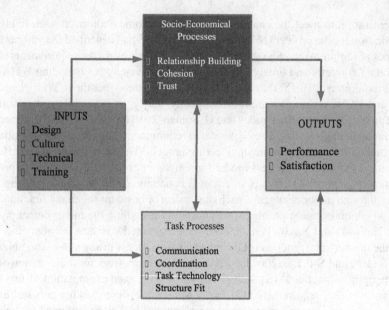

Fig. 1. General hierarchical structure of virtual environment

By using the general structure suggested by, Powell, Piccoli and Ives, a framework for managing functional requirements is suggested. According to this framework, the requirements should be prioritized by the manager at the beginning of the project, as clearly as possible so that each team member should be able to know the specific importance of each requirement as well as its overall priority in the project. The requirement of having the highest priority should be dealt with first. Following this framework, functional requirements can be managed more efficiently as shown in Fig. 1. (Fig. 2)

3.1 Proposed Framework

According to our proposed framework first when then-leader has prioritized the requirement already, so when the first requirement is considered, we will differentiate it into the functional and non-functional requirement, if it's a functional requirement then is a priority will be judged that either it's the highest priority requirement or not. If it's the highest priority requirement then the system will accept it and it will be executed otherwise, we will go back and check for the highest priority requirement again.

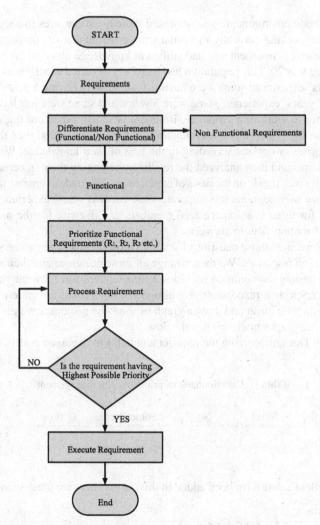

Fig. 2. Proposed framework flow chart

4 Result and Discussion

Although the use of virtual team will continue to grow. There are numerous challenges or issues to work in a virtual team. Our topic of discussion is how to manage the functional requirement of the software in a virtual team environment. To derive or suggest a solution, we did a survey. We made a questionnaire that included numerous questions (about 45–50) each question had four to five options. Few questions were generally about a virtual team environment few were about the issues and challenges faced in virtual environment, few questions were related to general requirement management, few were on functional requirement management, then some questions relating to the management of functional requirement, and lastly, some were on how the functional requirements can be managed using virtual team environment. we distributed these questionnaires to about 20 people who are either working currently in virtual team environment or somehow are linked with virtual team environment and had sufficient knowledge about it. So basically, our population size was 20. This population had members of varied experiences. Some were having 6 years' experience some were having 4, some were having 5 years' experience few were of 2 years' experience, some were 3 years, and some were just having a single year experience to work in a virtual environment. We distributed our questionnaire to this population they filled this questionnaire by marking the option they thought were the best responses or options according to the best of their knowledge. We recollected the questionnaires and then analyzed the results by arranging them in certain rows and columns. Tables were made on the basis of experiences. We made a separate table for one-year experience members, another separate table for two years' experience members, another table for three-year experienced members and likewise for the members who have worked for about four to six years.

Then we separated those questions for which most members or we can say majority gave the common responses. We then arrange all these questions and their responses in a table. After finding the common opinions we made graphs to show the percentage of responses by respective respondent. We assigned values to all the option, found their average or arithmetic mean and draw a graph to show the responses we got.

The data and graphs made are given below:

Statement: Does prioritizing the requirement helps in management? (Table 1)

Table 1. Questionnaire of prioritizing in management

Options	Never	No	Sometimes	Yes	Always
Assign values	1	2	3	4	5

20 respondent's data have been added in this survey; here are the responses of them.

Frequency values:
5,5,5,5,4,4,5,5,4,3,5,5,4,5,4,5,4,4,5,5

Respondent who strongly agree: 12
Total respondent: 20
Average = 12/20*100 = 60%
Respondent who agree: 7
Total respondent: 20
Average = 7/20*100 = 35%
Respondent who said sometimes: 1
Total respondent: 20
Average = 1/20*100 = 5%
Respondent who disagree (no): 0
Total respondent: 20
Average = 0/20*100 = 0%

Respondent who strongly disagree: 0
Total respondent: 20
Average = 0/20*100 = 0% (Fig. 3)

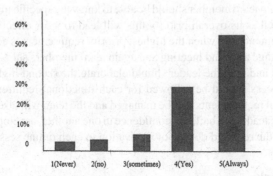

Fig. 3. Graph data for prioritizing the requirement helping in management

When we conducted this survey more than half i.e. about 60% of the population said that if we priorities the requirement it will help in overall management.

After considering all the data received by all the respondents, we have reached to a conclusion that 95% of the population said that functional requirement is of core importance in a life cycle of the product.55% said that they do face a change in requirement during the development process. 95% said that online meetings are worthy.65% said that sometimes they understand the requirement just through online meetings while sometimes not, the reason might be the language barrier. When we asked that what steps should be taken to cross the language barrier? 55% which means more than half of a population said more meetings should be conducted in order to cross language barrier. These more meetings will also help in developing understanding, trust and sense of team spirit among the virtual team members. When asked that do you think managing the requirement is more difficult in a virtual team environment. More than half of the population said "NO". 55% of members said that they do face a change in requirement during the development process.45% of members said that sometimes their company manages the requirement perfectly and sometimes not. A large portion of population that is 80% said that completing one task boosts up the confidence and spirit for the next task (or requirement).as team members will feel more confident and they will have the spirit of teamwork. 60%said that prioritizing the requirements at the very beginning of the project will aid in the efficient management of functional requirements. And lastly, 80% of the population strongly agreed the functional requirement with the highest priority should be dealt with first.

5   Conclusion

Considering all these facts and figures, after analyzing whole the statistical data we have concluded that to efficiently manage the functional requirement in a virtual team environment. The leader of the team should arrange the first online meeting or conference as soon as the team is chosen. In this very first meeting, every member should give a brief introduction about oneself so that a bit of a precise image of each member will be generated which could lead to building trust and confidence among team members. After the introduction the leader should prioritize the functional requirements as clearly as possible so that each team member should be able to know the specific importance of each requirement as well as its overall priority this will lead to more effective and managed functional requirements and when the highest priority requirement is accomplished, the leader should arrange a second meeting and again team members should have a fraction of time to discuss and then the leader should elaborate the second-highest requirement and the same process should be followed for each functional requirement. So, in this way, the functional requirements will be managed and the team will also feel the spirit of working in a team, leading to building confidence in one another, developing professional trust, and getting the required dosage of motivation in each online session or meeting.

6   Future Work

As this research focuses on the well manage functional requirement management, similarly in the future we can work to manage the non-functional requirements of a software project in a virtual team environment.

References

1. Li, Y., Li, H., Mädche, A., Rau, P.L.P.: Are you a trustworthy partner in a cross-cultural virtual environment? behavioral cultural intelligence and receptivity-based trust in virtual collaboration. In: Proceedings of the 4th International Conference on Intercultural Collaboration, pp. 87–96 (2012)
2. Kaushal, K., Richard, H., Dilanthi, A.: Achieving success in collaborative research: the role of virtual research environments. J. Inform. Technol. Constr. **14**, 59–69 (2009)
3. Powell, A., Piccoli, G., Ives, B.: Virtual teams: a review of current literature and directions for future research. ACM Sigmis Database **35**(1), 6–36 (2004)
4. Thamhain, H.J.: The role of team collaboration in complex product developments. In: Technology Management in the Energy Smart World (PICMET), 2011 Proceedings of PICMET'11, pp. 1–7 (2011)
5. Lai, R., Ali, N.: A requirements management method for global software development. Adv. Inform. Sci. **1**(1), 38–58 (2013)
6. Westfall, L.: Software requirements engineering what, why, who, when, and how. Softw. Qual. Prof. **7**(4), 17 (2005)
7. Pandey, D., Suman, U., Ramani, A.K.: An effective requirement engineering process model for software development and requirements management. In: Advances in Recent Technologies in Communication and Computing (ARTCom), 2010 International Conference on, pp. 287–291 (2010)
8. Kirkman, B.L., et al.: The impact of team empowerment on virtual team performance: the moderating role of face-to-face interaction. Acad. Manag. J. **47**(2), 175–192 (2004)
9. Dimovski, V., Penger, S.: Virtual management: a cross-section of the management process illustrating its fundamental functions of planning, organizing, leading and controlling in a new era organization. J. Bus. Econ. Res. **1**(10), 1–10 (2011)

10. Ebrahim, N.A., Ahmad, S., Taha, Z.: Virtual teams: a literature review. Aust. J. Basic Appl. Sci. **3**(3), 2653–2669 (2009)
11. Shi, L., Li, Z.: Research on the walkthrough engine for virtual environment. In: Proceedings of the IEEE 16th International Conference on Computer Supported Cooperative Work in Design, p. 591595 (2012)
12. Bavota, G., Lucia, A.D., Zottoli, C.: Teaching software engineering and software project management: an integrated and practical approach. In: Proceedings of the 34th International Conference on Software Engineering IEEE Press, pp. 1155–1164 (2012)
13. Maneva, N.: Software quality assurance and maintenance for outsourced software development. In: Proceedings of the First Balkan Conference on Informatics, pp. 21–23 (2003)
14. Viswanath, U.: Lean transformation: how lean helped to achieve quality, cost and schedule: case study in a multi location product development team. In: 2014 IEEE 9th International Conference on Global Software Engineering, pp. 95–99 (2014)
15. Sadana, V., Liu, X.F.: Analysis of conflicts among non-functional requirements using integrated analysis of functional and non-functional requirements. In: 31st Annual International Computer Software and Applications Conference (COMPSAC), pp. 215–218 (2007)

Quality Assessment Framework for IoT Based Systems for Agriculture Industry 4.0

Syed Ali Haider Naqvi[1]($\boxtimes$), Rafaqut Kazmi[2], and Erum Iftikhar[3]

[1] Department of Computer Science, The Islamia University of Bahawalpur, Bahawalpur, Pakistan
syedalihaider.ciit@gmail.com

[2] Department of Software Engineering, The Islamia University of Bahawalpur, Bahawalpur, Pakistan

[3] Higher Education Department, Lahore, Pakistan

Abstract. As world is transforming to digital era so agriculture tends towards the IoT based smart systems with smarts objects. Smart object helps in monitoring and performing smart actions according to situations without human intervention. Real time monitoring of agriculture fields requires efficient and reliable services for cost reduction, efficient management and making smart decisions. IoT, as a critical Industry 4.0 enabler emerges smart agriculture technologies for cost reduction, increase production and advanced Big data analytics for smart decisions for further improvements. However, the agriculture with limited resources is facing challenges to change the longstanding production and meet current requirements. This study aims to fulfil the gaps related to quality of system by transforming conventional agriculture to IoT-enabled smart systems. An industry-led study demonstrates how to make the reliable smart systems based on IoT technologies with emerging Industry 4.0 and improve the production rate to fulfill the current needs of era.

Keywords: Industry 4.0 · Smart agriculture · Internet of things · Cloud based IoT · Quality assessment framework · Reliability analysis

1 Introduction

The pervasiveness of internet from over the past two decades gave too many benefits to the organizations and citizens over the world. The real time services for the consumer and producer are the primary benefits of this revolution. The novel technologies of Internet of Things (IoT) embed the smartness in environment to enhance the user experience. According to MIT's researcher Kevin Ashton term presented in 1999 for objects connected through wireless technology and RFIF is "The Internet of Things". IoT introduced with the strong comprehensive view of connecting the globe, so that the people can easily get any type of service anywhere at any time. The multiplied exponential growth of IoT in last decade increase the number of connected objects on internet [1]. Now smart systems gain popularity due to huge range of networks, fusion of physical

© Springer Nature Switzerland AG 2022
D. N. A. Jawawi et al. (Eds.): ESMoC 2021, CCIS 1615, pp. 134–142, 2022.
https://doi.org/10.1007/978-3-031-19968-4_14

objects, IoT, Artificial Intelligence (AI), big data and cloud computing. The features of smart IoT are the autonomy, real time monitoring, optimization and controlling [2]. The notification system and monitoring dashboard is the direct and immediate advantage provided by IoT to the smart systems. In domain of retail, healthcare, security, traffic, smart cities, smart homes, and agriculture IoT provides various solutions.

The field of agriculture required continuous controlling and monitoring so deployment of IoT is ideal solution in this domain. In the agriculture industrial manufacture chain IoT deployed at various levels [3]. Greenhouse, livestock, and precision farming are the core applications of IoT in agriculture and these are classify in various monitoring areas. IoT based sensors and devices are used for monitoring of these application. The several technologies like actuators, embedded systems, sensors, web technologies, networks and wireless technologies are integrated for the formation of IoT based smart systems. All smart objects in IoT should have capabilities to interact and communication with each other and with other objects in IoT network and have unique identities [4].

1.1 Actuators and Sensors

The selection of actuators and sensors is application domain dependent. A huge amount of sensors are presented for various application domains, as Gas sensors for monitoring pollution (CO_2, O_2, CO, NO_2, SO_2, O_3, etc.), monitoring sensors for water quality (conductivity, pH, dissolved oxygen, etc.); general purpose sensors, e.g. pressure sensors, humidity, temperature, etc.; forest fires, etc.; and microphones and cameras.

1.2 Communication Technologies

Various standards and technologies have been presented for the communication capabilities e.g. 6LoWPAN, ZigBee, RFID (Radio Frequency Identification), Zwave, WiFi, Near Field Communication (NFC), WirelessHART, Bluetooth Low Energy, Ethernet, Mobile-phone technologies (2G/3G/4G), etc. The inexpensive microchips with distinctive identities and wireless communication capabilities are RFIDs. Several WSN solution have been presented based on 6LoWPAN, IEEE 802.15.4 standards, e.g. ZigBee etc.

1.3 Cloud Computing Technologies

For sharing the computing resources e.g. storage, server, applications, services, networks, etc. cloud computing technologies used. Platform as a Service (PaaS), Software as a Service (SaaS) and Infrastructure as a Service (IaaS) are the classes of clouds based on services, the classes of clouds based on ownership are community, public and private [5]. In cloud computing cloud platforms get sensor's data then analyze, interpret and store data; and also provide decision support visualization to the user [6].

1.4 IoT Framework for Agriculture Application

In the complete life cycle of agriculture sector (cultivation, harvest, water management, transportation, storage, sales and processing), the IoT application domains are ubiquitous with the availability of common and specialized sensors for smart agriculture applications, e.g. Ultraviolet Radiations, Leaf Wetness, Wind Vanes, Humidity, Soil moisture, Solar Radiations, Pluviometer (Rain Gauge), etc. Framework for IoT based agriculture system is shown through Fig. 1 [7].

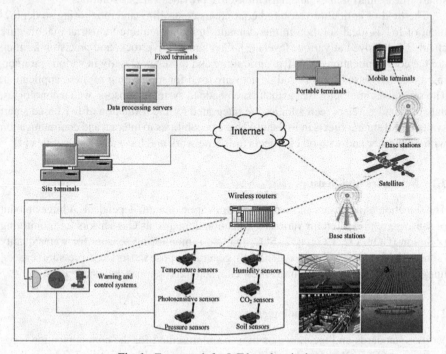

Fig. 1. Framework for IoT based agriculture

1.5   Quality for IoT Based Smart Agriculture

Being vital in development of IoT based Smart systems, quality is still a delicate term. According the state of the art [8], there are several ways to define quality:"meeting requirements" and"fitness for use". Both methodologies emphasis on the requirements and the level of fitting of the system with them. Nevertheless, last one, it is a wider definition broadening the meaning of quality to involve the user's (customer's) contentment. The quality of a software product is strongly reliant on the quality of the software system development methodology applied to develop that product [9, 10]. Quality model is a blend of different parameters as integrity, traceability, clarity of design, reliability and documentation, and associations among different components of system. These parameters define the quality of software products. Agriculture applications based on IoT technology required better quality to improve the production rate and for meeting the need. Reliability is the core component of quality of any system.

There are several methods to quantitatively assess the reliability quality of the IoT network [11–18]. Two main types are the experimental based and model based [19]. In experimental based approach reliability parameter of system can be precisely assessed through the recording of system parameter attributes and monitoring. In model-based approach reliability evaluation is done by using mathematical models and computer simulation or stochastic process. Experimental based approach is more realistic than the model-based approach but much time consuming for evaluating the reliability characteristics of system. For new system model-based techniques may get some upcoming reliability characteristics before development of system, some model-based approaches for assessment of reliability of IoT based systems are Markov chain [20], Fault tree analysis [21] and Reliability Block Diagram model [22]. The fusion of distinct models for evaluation can be used for better efficiency and accuracy [19]. For the technology-based system reliability is the probability of correct working of that system over a given period in planned environment [23].

Reliability is the ability of an item to perform a necessary function, under environmental and operational conditions over a defined period (ISO 8402) [24]. Item express the system and function express the service of that system. Main focus of earlier monitoring model is the availability of system where time between system failures is recorded for checking availability.

In this paper we introduced a reliability-based quality assessment framework for IoT based agriculture on the base of quality parameters including robustness and reliability in context of failure.

The rest of paper is organized in five sections, section two address the related work.

Section three represents the proposed framework and section four shows the results. At the end in section five whole study is concluded.

2 Related Work

Monitoring and KM-Knowledge based framework for e-Agriculture application proposed in [25] to facilitate the farmers by helping for making profitable decisions through providing required information to farmer during the complete farming cycle. An Agricultural IoT Reference Architecture (AITRA) proposed in [26] which consist of three layers: business, cloud and device. The applications of IoT techniques in agriculture summarized in [7] which includes four categories: live-stock breeding open field planting, controlled environment planting, and aquaponics and aquaculture. The main discussed concerns include agriculture products life cycle, energy, IoT finance and management issue. Various services are embedding in IoT which increasing the risks of smart systems. The interconnection of diverse heterogenous devices boost up the scalability problems which required the flexibility in system. A cross domain prototype architecture is proposed in [27] to manage the quality issues. Reliability analysis of non-banking financial institutions is presented in [28] which improves the relationship with customer, so the cloud service provider and users are the key component of reliability of cloud service. In computer network end to end reliability improve the system's performance. The reliability features of two IoT architectures evaluated in [19] with main network parameters using OPNET and with the increasing sensor nodes in IoT network the reliability effected analyzed by simulation.

The systems based on Wireless Sensor Network (WSN) are heterogenous and incompatible so there is lack of coordination between processes and regions. A system for oil and gas industry based on IoT presented in [29] for reliable, robust and secure communication and can be implement on downstream, upstream and midstream operations. To get rid of complex device programming and configurations, cloud technologies and IoT based smart objects are used. A number of sensors are required for gathering data in IoT application and the most critical requirements of WSN are the resilience, reliability and energy conservation. In the context of failures resilience and reliability ensured by the fault tolerance. A fault tolerant approached for WSN in IoT network is proposed in [30] which improves the reliability of IoT based smart system. With the technological advancement computational power increases and rich data generation taking spike so the sophisticated models for computation are implemented to advance the estimation of device failures in context of reliability of system [31]. A systematic framework presented in [32] that integrates a sensor-driven predictive approach and a resourceful preservation policy. The predictive approach uses deprivation indications for every machine to update and predicts its failure time and the system level maintenance done with respect to real time.

3   Proposed Model

IoT based architecture for smart agriculture systems is shown in Fig. 2. Field divided into three parts for placing sensors as front, middle and end of the field and every part has one node. Each of the nodes has sensors including air, temperature, humidity, soil and light intensity sensors. Data sensed through the sensor and processed the controlled by the primary controlling node. Sensed data will be sent to cloud of IoT for analysis purpose and then after analysis data sent back to the controller.

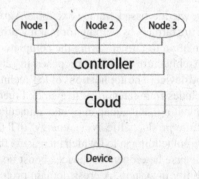

Fig. 2. IoT based smart agriculture system

3.1   Parameters for Reliability

- Rate of failure
- Collected data
- Data Processing and communication speed

3.2 Quality Assessment Framework

Proposed quality assessment framework for IoT based smart systems for agriculture industry 4.0 in context of reliability consist of three parts as: monitor, dependency analysis and reliability analysis as shown by Fig. 3.

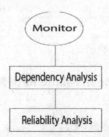

Fig. 3. Quality assessment framework

Monitor step capture the status and register the smart system's breakdowns and report send to dependency analyzer. Dependency analyzer receives report and creates dependency graph through cloud manager. In reliability analysis the reliability analyzer checks all objects for the sake of trust and failure rate to achieve better quality of the smart system in IoT environment.

4 Experimentation

IoT based architecture was developed and installed for small sized field. The data transmission among the components monitored for two months. The mean values of Mean Time Between Failures and failure computed. The experimental outcomes are shown in Table 1 and illustrated by Fig. 4 and 5. Due to low-cost sensor the annual mean failures are assessed based on two months. Several factors influenced the failure characteristics of IoT cloud.

The experimental outcomes shows that the sensor unit has higher mean failure rate and the controller node has less failure than the sensor as shown in Fig. 4. The cloud component in IoT network is the not failed most of the operating time span. The cause behind it the standard cloud service providers who gives high performance computing facility with backup. Nevertheless, outcomes shows that failure of any component may fail the whole system so the reliability of system depend on reliability of its components.

The exploratory outcomes confirmed that the IoT framework with longer data transmission way would have less reliability. In any case, for this situation, the general system quality isn't essentially extraordinary.

Additionally, the applied IoT worker has exceptionally high reliability. Subsequently, the IoT correspondence design might be appropriate for a little estimated framework with less computational investigation. Notwithstanding, framework dependability will be altogether diminished while expanding the quantity of sensors in light of the fact that the sensor has the low quality in this system.

Table 1. Mean MTBF and failure values

| | Values | |
	Mean failure rate %	Mean MBTF rate (Hrs.)
Sensors	0.132	700
Controller	0.016	6000
Cloud	0.00497	20000

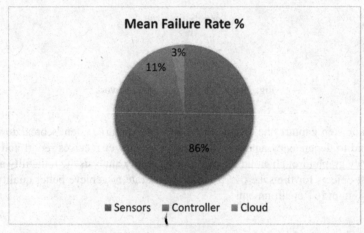

Fig. 4. Mean failure rate

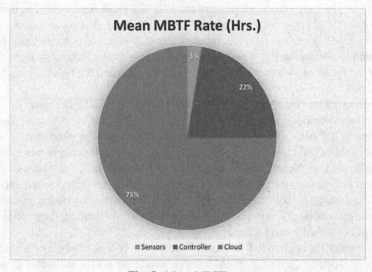

Fig. 5. Mean MBTF rate

In addition, moving the computational ability onto the cloud can without much of a stretch deal with the multifaceted nature of the data examination and reduce the outstanding task at hand of the microcontroller. Nonetheless, a good internet is required for data transmission.

5 Conclusion

This research demonstrates the quality assessment of the IoT based communication architectures for agriculture. The outcomes of the reliability parameters (MTBF and Failure) have been examining and assessed from the real experimentation. Then the reliability of is computed and the outcomes demonstrates that the IoT communication architecture based on cloud technology would be the best way for small or medium-sized farming. This due to the system reliability characteristics. Nevertheless, cloud-based architecture can provide better performance and scalability for industry 4.0 based agriculture. Proposed quality assessment framework can be utilized for other IoT based systems.

References

1. Patel, C., Doshi, N.: A novel MQTT security framework in generic IoT model. Procedia Comput. Sci. **171**, 1399–1408 (2020)
2. Aheleroff, S., et al.: IoT-enabled smart appliances under industry 4.0: a case study. Adv. Eng. Inform. **43**, 101043 (2020)
3. Medela, A., Cendón, B., González, L., Crespo, R., Nevares, I.: IoT multiplatform networking to monitor and control wineries and vineyards. In: 2013 Future Network & Mobile Summit, pp. 1–10 (2013)
4. Miorandi, D., Sicari, S., De Pellegrini, F., Chlamtac, I.: Internet of things: vision, applications and research challenges. Ad hoc Netw. **10**(7), 1497–1516 (2012)
5. Botta, A., de Donato, W., Persico, V., Pescapé, A.: Integration of cloud computing and internet of things: a survey. Future Gener. Comput. Syst. **56**, 684–700 (2016)
6. Gubbi, J., Buyya, R., Marusic, S., Palaniswami, M.: Internet of Things (IoT): a vision, architectural elements, and future directions. Future Gener. Comput. Syst. **29**(7), 1645–1660 (2013). https://doi.org/10.1016/j.future.2013.01.010
7. Ruan, J., et al.: A life cycle framework of green IoT-based agriculture and its finance, operation, and management issues. IEEE Commun. Mag. **57**(3), 9096 (2019)
8. Committee, I.S.C.: IEEE Standard Glossary of Software Engineering Terminology (IEEE Std 610.12-1990), vol. 169. IEEE Computer Society, Los Alamitos. CA (1990)
9. Akbar, M.A., et al.: Statistical analysis of the effects of heavyweight and lightweight methodologies on the six-pointed star model. IEEE Access **6**, 8066–8079 (2018)
10. Kroeger, T.A., Davidson, N.J., Cook, S.C.: Understanding the characteristics of quality for software engineering processes: a grounded theory investigation. Inf. Softw. Technol. **56**(2), 252–271 (2014)
11. Silva, I., Leandro, R., Macedo, D., Guedes, L.A.: A dependability evaluation tool for the Internet of Things. Comput. Electr. Eng. **39**(7), 2005–2018 (2013)
12. Macedo, D., Guedes, L.A., Silva, I.: A dependability evaluation for Internet of Things incorporating redundancy aspects. In: Proceedings of the 11th IEEE international conference on networking, sensing and control, IEEE (2014)

13. Bo, Y., Wang, H.: The application of cloud computing and the internet of things in agriculture and forestry. In: 2011 International Joint Conference on Service Sciences. IEEE (2011)
14. Kamyod, C., Nielsen, R.H., Prasad, N.R., Prasad, R.: End-to-end availability analysis of IMS-based networks: simplex and redundant systems. In: 2013 IEEE Wireless Communications and Networking Conference (WCNC), pp. 1103–1108 (2013)
15. Kamyod, C., Nielsen, R.H., Prasad, N.R., Prasad, R.: IMS intra- and inter domain end-to-end resilience analysis. In: Wireless VITAE 2013, pp. 1–5 (2013)
16. Kamyod, C., Nielsen, R.H., Prasad, N.R., Prasad, R.: Resilience of the IMS system: the resilience effect of inter-domain communications. In: 2014 4th International Conference on Wireless Communications, Vehicular Technology, Information Theory and Aerospace & Electronic Systems (VITAE), pp. 1–4 (2014)
17. Kamyod, C.: Reliability analysis of an e-learning network: a case study of Mae Fah Luang University. In: 2017 International Conference on Digital Arts, Media and Technology (ICDAMT), pp. 389–391 (2017)
18. Kamyod, C., Nielsen, R., Prasad, N., Prasad, R., Aunsri, N.: End-to-end reliability and optimization of intra and inter-domain IMS-based communication networks. J. Cyber Secur. Mobility 5(3), 233–256 (2017)
19. Kamyod, C.: End-to-end reliability analysis of an IoT based smart agriculture. In: 2018 International Conference on Digital Arts, Media and Technology (ICDAMT). IEEE (2018)
20. Li, L., Jin, Z., Li, G., Zheng, L., Wei, Q.: Modeling and analyzing the reliability and cost of service composition in the IoT: a probabilistic approach. In: 2012 IEEE 19th International Conference on Web Services, pp. 584–591 (2012)
21. Kabir, S.: An overview of fault tree analysis and its application in model based dependability analysis. Expert Syst. Appl. 77, 114–135 (2017)
22. Azghiou, K., El Mouhib, M., Koulali, M.-A., Benali, A.: An end-to-end reliability framework of the internet of things. Sensors 20(9), 2439 (2020)
23. Kirkman, R.A.: Failure concepts in reliability theory. IEEE Trans. Reliab. 12(4), 1–10 (1963)
24. Souza, M.L.H., da Costa, C.A., de Oliveira Ramos, G., da Rosa Righi, R.: A survey on decision-making based on system reliability in the context of Industry 4.0. J. Manuf. Syst. 56, 133–156 (2020)
25. Mohanraj, I., Ashokumar, K., Naren, J.: Field monitoring and automation using IOT in agriculture domain. Procedia Comput. Sci. 93, 931–939 (2016)
26. El-Basioni, B.M.M., Abd El-Kader, S.M.: Laying the foundations for an IoT reference architecture for agricultural application domain. IEEE Access 8, 190194190230 (2020)
27. Sicari, S., Rizzardi, A., Miorandi, D., Cappiello, C., Coen-Porisini, A.: A secure and quality-aware prototypical architecture for the Internet of Things. Inform. Syst. 58, 43–55 (2016)
28. Rajini, S.N.S., Ramamoorthy, S., Radha Rammohan, S., Rajakumar, P.S., Niveditha, V.R.: Reliability of cloud services provided to non-banking financial institutions. Int. J. Control Autom. 13(2s), 165–172 (2020)
29. Khan, W.Z., Aalsalem, M.Y., Khan, M.K., Hossain, M.S., Atiquzzaman, M.: A reliable Internet of Things based architecture for oil and gas industry. In: 2017 19th International Conference on Advanced Communication Technology (ICACT), pp. 705–710 (2017)
30. Muhammed, T., Mehmood, R., Albeshri, A.: Enabling reliable and resilient IoT based smart city applications. In: International Conference on Smart Cities, Infrastructure, Technologies and Applications. Springer (2017)
31. Sahal, R., Breslin, J.G., Ali, M.I.: Big data and stream processing platforms for Industry 4.0 requirements mapping for a predictive maintenance use case. J. Manuf. Syst. 54, 138–151 (2020)
32. Xia, T., Fang, X., Gebraeel, N., Xi, L., Pan, E.: Online analytics framework of sensor-driven prognosis and opportunistic maintenance for mass customization. J. Manuf. Sci. Eng. 141(5), 051011 (2019)

CMMI Software Evolution and Its Role in Pakistan

Atif Ali[✉]

PMAS Arid Agriculture University, Rawalpindi, Pakistan
atif.alii@yahoo.com

Abstract. Software evolution is a process that is a current need of the software industry and software users, either it is an organization or an individual. In this paper, an analysis of different things related to software evolution will be seen. It is a study towards some mature software evolution process which Capability Maturity Model Integration (CMMI). We will see an aspect of software evolution in Pakistan. CMMI history will be under the discussion of how it evolves and the benefits of using it. We will make a comparison of different evolution process models with CMMI to have a look at its competencies. We will have a view of Lehman Law and finally CMMI involvement in the Pakistan software industry. Section 1 will be the Introduction and the importance of software evolution in Pakistan. Section 2 CMMI History will be discussed, and Sect. 3, depicts CMMI Comparison. Section 4.1 will introduce Lehman Law, and finally, Sect. 5 is Analysis.

Keywords: CMMI · Software evolution · Lehman law · Requirement changes

1 Introduction

Software is a current need and the right solution all over the world. But a reason for failure is the main reason for lacking confidence in software solutions. Some of the causes of failure of software are. Incorrect data collection, low requirement gathering, Not acquiring the whole piece of the required information, Sudden change/s in requirements/planned solution, Inadequate fund flow, Volatile resources, bad social influence [1]. Close to one-third of multi-billion dollar World Bank (WB) financed projects in Pakistan failed to achieve intended results, as was revealed by official archives available to the News from the Ministry of Economic Affairs, Economic Affairs Division. These exclusive archives suggest a steady rise in the number of failed projects for the past several years. A wholesome portfolio assessment of the WB funded projects in Pakistan shows that millions of dollars worth of individual projects like the Federal Board of Revenue's (FBR) Tax Administration Reform Project (TARP); the Project to Improve Financial Reporting and Auditing (PIFRA), and numerous public sector capacity building and the WB funded improvement projects. The funding amount in several of the projects mentioned above may be less, but the impact on severing key reforms remained massive [2].

D. N. A. Jawawi et al. (Eds.): ESMoC 2021, CCIS 1615, pp. 143–153, 2022.
https://doi.org/10.1007/978-3-031-19968-4_15

The audit and accountability option available to the deprived owners of resources was to approach a WB. Inspection Panel, and that is what they did. With concerns and complaints of rights violations of the resource owners, the results of a series of investigations backed up several communities' claims that how irresponsibly WB played havoc with community members' daily livelihood. The investigation also revealed flaws in technical designs. The investigation into social effects on the community exposed fifty-four breach occurrences at different locations resulting in life losses to neighboring communities. Additionally, several issues concerning environmental problems, slow management administration were also identified [3].

Lack of comprehension of User Requirements; lack of Change Control Mechanism; Lack of effective Testing Methodology; Lack of user involvement (from requirements gathering to final product deployment); Unrealistic and/or long timescale; and Scope Creep are significant factors that have historically affected and contributed massively towards project success or failure. Many studies and reports have placed the six factors mentioned earlier, at the top or near-top of this list [5]. In [6], research is conducted on projects undergone in some institutions, i.e., National Institute of Public.

Administration (NIPA's), Pakistan Academy of Rural Development (PARD), National Center of Rural Development (NCRD), National Defense College (NDC), Pakistan Management Institute (PMI) and more, and opinions of individuals from the federal and provincial government and private. They have firm experience in their fields. This research finds some weak areas which need to be reformed or enhanced: Project Identification, Project Preparation, Project Authorization, Project Implementation, Project Evaluation, Policy Perceptions. The research findings suggested several issues being faced by the OGDCL in effective project management. Several project managers agree that most clients either lack visibility of project development/management related problems or cannot clearly express their requirements, leading to a lack of understanding of the project managers' part. Another glaring issue faced was regarding the difference of opinions between project managers and clients. The latter also agree that the lack of requisite funds and resources necessary for the project's continuity and momentum significantly hindered the progress and presented a significant drag factor. However, project management conception results remained satisfactory, which shows that most of the managers have requisite know-how regarding project management's core concepts. Adding on, many project managers concurred on the fact that there are no pre-defined set of procedures to prevent projects from missing deadlines/targets/milestones. Building on this, many project managers were unaware of any backup plan regarding how the lagging project can be brought back on a satisfactory progress track [7]. One of the negative impacts observed in concurrently running projects was that it slowed down the projects' pace. The majority of managers agreed that the management of concurrent projects requires a higher level of skillset. Another issue is related to employee performance management. Some recommendations are Risk Identification, Risk Quantification, Risk Prioritization, Risk Response, Risk Monitoring & Control [7].

As noted earlier, the reasons for IT projects' failure in the developing and developed world are nearly identical. It also includes Pakistan. The claim is not being made based on any evidence supporting this, as no such study/report has been published so far. However, it can very well be deduced due to many similarities in developing countries' circumstances like lack of quality education and IT skills development facilities, unstable political and economic conditions, lack of certified software houses, and stakeholders' reluctance to invest automated business solutions, etc. Ownership of the Project,

Unrealistic Expectations, Stakeholder Politics, Team Building Issues, Communication and Issues, Conflict among top Management, Budgetary Issues, Neglect of Project Risk Management, Resistance Issues, Maturity Levels of IT Pakistan [7].

2 CMMI History Trail

The quality of a (software) system is dictated by the quality of processes used for its development and subsequent maintenance. Capability Maturity Model (CMM) was developed as an inspiration and amalgam of different quality measures including, but not limited to, Total Quality Management (TQM), Crosby's Maturity Grid, IBM's Process Grid. The evolution of CMM in different eras is because of the dissatisfaction of its usage concerns. Issues like Questionnaire as Model, Level of Abstraction, Scoring, Reliability & Consistency, SCE Team Training, Level of Detail, Availability of Training, Management of Software Process, Issues with Domains, Usability, Scope, Requirements Elicitation, an Audit Checklist, Customer's Maturity, Maintenance, Appraiser Qualifications, Focusing on Level Number, Source of Change, etc. mature a process model from CMM to CMMI. See Table1 for History Detail [8].

Table 1 Continuous and Staged Architecture Models leading to CMMI [8]

Year	Model
1979	Crosby's maturity grid (Quality is Free)
1985	IBM maturity grid (Radice)
1987	SEI software process maturity framework
1988	SEI software process domains
1989	SEI normative model
1990	SEI Software CMM v0.2
1990	SEI Software CMM v0.6
1991	SEI Software CMM v1.0
1993	SEI Software CMM v1.1
1995	SPICE Baseline Practices Guide
1995	Systems Engineering CMM
1997	SEI Software CMM v2 Draft C
1998	EIA 731 (Systems Engineering Capability Model)
1998	ISO/IEC 15,504 type 2 technical reports
2000	SEI CMM Integration v1.0 (both)

A list of benefits such as risk management, engineering management, organizational criticality and concerns, detailed coverage of product life cycle, a combination of product engineering and proven practices, and much more are a consideration in terms of benefits of CMMI.

A mature CMMI is compiled on 5 levels: Initial, Repeatable, Defined, Managed, and Optimized. To move from Level 1 to 2, key actions are Project Management, Management Oversight, Product Assurance, and Change Control. From Level 2 to 3, the actions involved are Process Group, Process Architecture, and Software Engineering methods. For Level 4, the key actions are Process Measurement, Process Database, Process Analysis, and Product Quality. To achieve Level 5, the concerns include Automated Support and Process Optimization [9]. CMMI chief architect Roger Bate explains,

> *"Integrating process improvement models is no easy task. The CMMI project's source models use different approaches and architectures, and they cover some different topics. The CMMI product development team, as diverse as it is, achieved consensus on many tough issues. The result is a set of process improvement models that can meet the needs of many organizations now and can grow to meet the needs of more organizations in the future."*

The demand for better integration of CMM models where created opportunities, also presented several challenges relevant to better training and assessment methods. To address this, the United States Department of Defence (Office of the Undersecretary of Defence for Acquisition & Sustainment OUD A&S) in close collaboration with the National Defence Industrial Association (NDIA) led the Capability Maturity Model Integration (CMMI) initiative. Several experts from different backgrounds and organizations were asked to build a wholesome framework that should encompass current and future models [10]. Following benefits are expected to be accrued from the use of CMMI models:

- Cost reduction
- Improved predictability of project costs and schedules
- Higher quality and rate of productivity
- Shorter cycle time
- Increased customer satisfaction
- Higher employee morale

CMMI has five Levels to be accomplished as a complete process improvement architecture implementation. Each level has a Key Process Areas (KPA). There are key process areas (KPAs) within each of these maturity levels that characterize that level, and five measures for each KPA:

- Goals
- Commitment
- Ability
- Measurement
- Verification

CMMI models are used today by organizations from private, public, and government sectors to effect process improvements in integrated products and processes development process, Systems Engineering integration methods, and Software Engineering processes. Organizations use the processes to help them develop, acquire, maintain products and services, and benchmark themselves against others. Better processes lead to reduced costs and better-quality results, and more realistic timing estimates for projects [11].

What improvements can I expect? Table 2 from the SEI website contains a summary of the performance results reported by 25 organizations, stated in terms of performance change over time.

Table 2. CMMI implementation results [11]

Performance category	Median	Number of data points	Low	High
Cost	20%	21	3%	87%
Schedule	37%	19	2%	90%
Productivity	62%	17	9%	255%
Quality	50%	20	7%	132%
Customer satisfaction	14%	6	− 4%	55%
Return on investment	4.7:1	16	2:1	27.7:1

Senior executives proclaimed increased levels of confidence, which was based on the achievement of consistency. According to them, the resultant confidence did not even require level 5 Maturity levels. Even executives from companies at maturity levels 2 and 3 reflected boosted satisfaction with how developments are now on time, on budget, and the customers were delighted [11].

3 CMMI Comparison

An essential aspect of evaluating local practices for software evolution is identifying opportunities as to where new and useful technologies can be employed. New software engineering tools, techniques, or management strategies are introduced during the middle of a system development effort in many situations. There are many life cycle models for software engineering, including [12]:

- Traditional Software Life Cycle Models ○ Classic Software Life Cycle ○ Refinement and Iterative Enhancement ○ Incremental Release ○ Industrial Practices and Military Standards
- Alternative Life Cycle Models ○ Software Product Development Models

  - Prototyping
  - Assembling Reusable Componentry
  - Application Generation

- Program Evolution Models ○ Software Production Process Model
- Non-Operational Process Models

- The Spiral Model
- Continuous Transformation Models
- Miscellaneous Process Models

  - Operational Process Models

    - Operational specifications for rapid prototyping
    - Software process automation and programming
    - Knowledge-based software automation ○ Software Production Setting Model

  - Software Project Management process models
  - Organizational Software Development models
  - Customer resource life cycle models
  - Software Transfer of Technology & Transition models
  - Other models for the organization of System Manufacturing & Production

    - Ad-hoc problem solving, tinkering, and articulation work
    - Group project
    - Custom job shop
    - Batched production
    - Pipeline
    - Flexible manufacturing systems
    - Transfer (assembly) lines
    - Continuous process control

Findings in comparison of these evolutionary processes are [12]:

- Evolution with testable predictions, no uncertainty is encountered.
- Stability is the concern of one or more process measure variables across different data sets.
- They cannot predict what will happen in different life cycle stages, different circumstances, or different kinds of software systems.
- The generality of their results I accessed from their sample space.
- They did not define what they want to accomplish from the process model.

Understanding the global software process and its global feedback structure has led to lesser details incorporation in the models than others and the consideration of long-term multirelease processes rather than single development cycles. Business constraints are applied to the process according to the type of environment, along with varying release patterns. Different sources of feedback become input factors to evolution, which affect the intended and applied use of the software. Differences in product attributes are due to:

- The level of product maturity
- Type of software product and
- Type of application [13].

Due to the small sample sizes created by focusing on system releases as the units of analyses, prior researchers have generally been limited in achieving a certain level of sophistication. This means that typically, only single variable OLS regression models have been estimated. Exceptions to this, including Yuen, employ time series analysis on more massive data sets. Generally, a few results were generated by Yuen's time-series analyses. (Some possible reasons for this are suggested in the results section of the current paper) [14].

The research in Software Evolution is a relatively younger field that continually keeps shifting focus and even the underlying core concepts. Everyone agrees on the need and inevitability of software evolution but modeling the evolution process is not easy due to increasingly complex environments in which software is designed, developed, and deployed. There still are many unanswered questions, answers to which need to be explored. Several research challenges lie ahead including, but not limited to, the problems of model building and empirical studies; the applicability of studying open source development; the modeling of emergent designs; improvements in the collective memory of developers through better artifact linkages; the emergence of software ecospheres; and the study and modeling of economic trade-offs and risks [15] (Fig. 1).

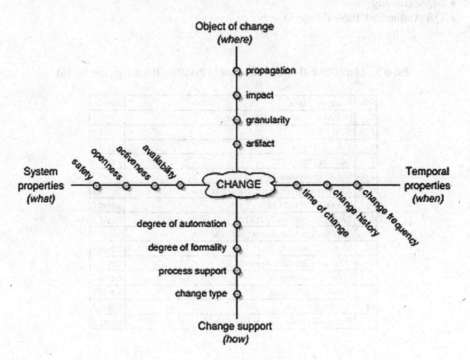

Fig. 1. Dimensions of software evolution [16]

4   CMMI in Pakistan

A survey was conducted to gauge. Out of 70 respondents, 45 are classified as "more experienced" firms. Out of these, 15 firms develop software for internal use, whereas the rest develop software for commercial use. Similarly, among 25 less experienced firms, 7 develop software for internal use and 18 for commercial use. Comparison of more experienced versus less experienced firms; Differences concerning the critical factors of quality and internal use versus external use; Differences concerning the critical quality factors [17].

The firms that participated in the research were classified into different groups based on "age of quality" and "use of the software." The results of the analyses performed in this study indicate that the "age of quality" in the Pakistan software industry has minimal influence over Software Quality Assurance. Only 2 out of 6 factors, i.e., Quality Certification (QC) and Automated Tools (AT), were found significant between "more experienced" firms versus "less experienced" firms. This indicates that there is not much difference present between "more experienced" and "less experienced" firms concerning critical factors of quality [17].

- % Investment on SQA
- Quality Certification
- Strength of SQA staff
- SQA Training
- QA Automated Tools (Table 3)

Table 3. List of CMMI rated companies in Pakistan: Extracted from [9, 18]

SNo	Company Name	Level
1	NetSol Technologies (Pvt.) Ltd.	Level 5
2	NCR Pakistan	Level 5
3	Kalsoft (Pvt.) Ltd.	Level 3
4	Systems (Pvt.) Ltd.	Level 3
5	Digital Processing Systems	Level 3
6	ZTE Pakistan, Software R & D Center	Level 2
7	Eworx Intl (Pvt.) Ltd.	Level 2
8	Techlogix Pakistan (Pvt.) Ltd.	Level 2
9	Si3 - System Innovations (Pvt.) Ltd.	Level 2
10	Abacus Consulting (Pvt.) Ltd.	Level 2
11	Descon Information Systems	Level 2
12	E-Dev Technologies	Level 2
13	Prosol Technologies	Level 2
14	Avanza Solutions	Level 2
15	Shaukat Khanum Cancer Research Hospital (IT DIV)	Level 2

The study found that the concept of standardization is not new in Pakistan. However, the culture's new orientation has shifted focus more towards smooth development processes and delivering better quality products. Simultaneously, the current situation, economic crises, and lack of awareness in terms of quality (CMM and CMMI) are negatively affecting Pakistan's image and have been a significant drag factor to the pace of growth [18].

The model to study the evolvement of commitment through the commitment process concentrates on the "How" aspect of top management commitment for TQM process implementation. To enhance commitment visibility in the TQM process is not an easy job. Quality philosophies about commitment are easy to preach but challenging to implement [19]. Outcomes are:

- There is a written TQM policy.
- Managers attend TQM meetings.
- There are written TQM goals and objectives.
- Managers participate in executing TQM plans.
- Managers monitor and periodically evaluate the TQM program.
- Managers regularly attend TQM activities outside the company.
- Managers provide TQM budgets, staffing, and facilities for meetings.
- Managers and supervisors are held accountable for TQM performance.
- Top managers receive and respond to TQM committee recommendations.
- Supervisors and managers personally conduct TQM audits and inspections.
- Management representatives are members of the TQM Committee/Team.
- Written strategies and tactics (plans) for achieving TQM objectives are in place.

A comprehensive structure to build a software house or make an existing one as a better solution provides a small business solution that is a good one to adopt [20].

4.1 LEHMAN LAW

"Evolution is an essential property of real-world software," and *"As your needs change, your criteria for satisfaction change."*

Lehman discovered that programmers were becoming increasingly interested in assessing their productivity, measured in terms of daily SLOCs, and passing unit-tests. Lehman's Law, presented first in 1974 three Laws [17–19], i.e.

- Law of Continuing Change
- Law of increasing entropy
- Law of statistically smooth growth

Lehman evolved in 1978 after sufficient industrial experience was acquired. The reformed law presented as:

- Law of Continuing Change
- Law of increasing complexity
- Law of statistically regular growth
- Law of invariant work rate

- Law of incremented growth limit

    In 1994, a revised form of Lehman's law presented as:

- Continuing change
- Increasing complexity
- Self-regulation
- Conservation of organizational stability
- Conservation of familiarity
- Continuing growth
- Declining quality
- Feedback system

5 Analysis

PSEB surveyed to gauge the benefits accrued by IT companies from the practice of CMMI. The survey results indicate the following statistics (Table 4):

Table 4. Extracted from [21]

Impact of CMMI		
Growth of HR strength	31.60%	36.27%
Employee retention rate	71.77%	82.73%
Reduction in project rework	38.67%	19.36%
Reduction in project delays	34.64%	16.35%
Export revenue	50.00%	65.98%
Domestic revenue	35.00%	146.59%

    After completing two CMMI programs, PSEB is now planning to launch phase-III of the subject program under the Ministry of Information Technology's auspices. The results of these two projects are as follows [22]:

- One company achieved CMMI Level 5.
- Four companies achieved CMMI Level 3.
- Eighteen companies achieved CMMI Level 2.

References

1. www.sei.cmu.edu/cmm/slides/cmm-historyhandout.pdf
2. Sahibzada, S.A., Mehmood, M.A.: Why most development projects fail in Pakistan? A plausible explanation. Pakistan Dev. Rev. **31**(4 Part II) 1111–1122 (1992)

3. http://www.sei.cmu.edu/library/abstracts/news-atsei/backgrounddec99.cfm. Accessed on 16 Aug 2014
4. http://www.cio.com/article/2437864/processimprovement/capability-maturity-model-integr ation-cmmi--definition-and-solutions.html. Accessed on 16 Aug 2014
5. Urkude, M.G., Urkude, A.M.: Why projects fail around the world? The reasons and concern http://www.indianmba.com/Faculty_Column/FC907/fc907.html. Accessed on 18 Aug 2014
6. Haider, M.: World Bank projects failing in Pakistan (2013). http://www.thenews.com.pk/Tod aysNews-3-206159-World-Bank-projects-failing-inPakistan
7. Mustafa Talpur with A. Porcelain and M. Nauman.: The World Bank in Pakistan: see no suffering, hear no cries, speak no truth. http://www.thenews.com.pk/Todays-News-3-206159 World-Bank-projects-failing-in-Pakistan
8. Why Projects Fail. http://www.coleyconsulting.co.uk/failure.htm. Accessed on 18 Aug 2014
9. Top Management Commitment for TQM – A Process Model. In: Pakistan 10th International Convention on Quality Improvement, Lahore (2006)
10. Small and Medium Enterprises Development Authority Government of Pakistan: Pre-feasibility study "Software House" www.smeda.org.pk. http://blogs.pseb.org.pk/general/, http://www.pseb.org.pk/pseb-programs/projects.html. Accessed on 16 Aug 2014
11. Aslam, S., Shah, S., Zaman, K., Hamid, Z., Musharraf.: Practical implication issues of project management in Oil and Gas Development Company Limited (OGDCL) Pakistan. J. Int. Acad. Res. 11(2) (2011)
12. Majeed, N., Shah, K.A., Qazi, K.A., Maqsood, M.: Performance evaluation of I.T project management in developing countries. Int. J. Inf. Technol. Comput. Sci. 4, 68–75 (2013)
13. Paulk, M.C.: Lecture: A History of the Capability Maturity Model for Software. Software Engineering Institute, Carnegie Mellon University: (Extracted from various resources)
14. Kieran Doyle, L.: The Role of CMMI. http://www.bcs.org/content/conWebDoc/7878. Accessed on 16 Aug 2014
15. Scacchi, W.: Models of Software Evolution: Life Cycle and Process SEI Curriculum Module SEI-CM-10-1.0. Carnegie Mellon University, Software Engineering Institute, Oct (1987)
16. Lehman, M., Wernick, P.: System Dynamics Models of Software Evolution Processes (1990)
17. Kemerer, C.F., Slaughter, S.: An empirical approach to studying software evolution. IEEE Trans. Softw. Eng. 25(4) (1999)
18. Godfrey, M.W., German, D.M.: The past, present, and future of software evolution. Mens, T., Buckley, J., Zenger, M., Rashid, A. Towards a Taxonomy of Software Evolution
19. Iftikhar, A., Ali, S.M.: Software Quality Assurance A Study Based on Pakistan's Software Industry
20. Hashmi, A.A., Mansoor, A., Khokhar, N.: Quantitative analysis of SPI in Pakistan. Int. J. Comput. Elect. Eng. 5(5) (2013)
21. https://sas.cmmiinstitute.com/pars/pars.aspx 2012, 2013, 2014
22. http://howpk.com/list-top-software-houses-pakistan/. Accessed on 17 Aug 2014
23. http://www.sochnews.tv/2014/04/top-10-best-softwarehouses-pakistan/. Accessed on 17 Aug 2014
24. http://blogs.pseb.org.pk/general/psebs-futureinitiatives/ or http://www.pseb.org.pk/pseb-pro grams/projects.html 2004 – 2006 by PSEB
25. http://spiresources.blogspot.com/2009/11/cmmicompanies-in-pakistan.html (2009)
26. http://www.tezimandee.com/forum/topic/420-netsolnetsol-technologie/page__st__2615 (2010)
27. http://www.khuram-shahzad.com/forum/discussion4836/Top-five-IT-companies,-Software-exporters-inthe-Lahore,-Punjab-Pakistan (2011)

Secure Software Development: Infuse Cyber Security to Mitigate Attacks in an Organization

Atif Ali[1(✉)], Yasir Khan Jadoon[2], Muhammad Qasim[3], Muhammad Shahid Iqbal[1], Asma[4], and Muhammad Usama Nazir[5]

[1] PMAS Arid Agriculture University, Rawalpindi, Pakistan
atif.alii@yahoo.com
[2] NUST University, Islamabad, Pakistan
[3] University of Wales, Cardiff, UK
[4] Riphah International University, Islamabad, Pakistan
[5] University of Central Punjab, Lahore, Pakistan

Abstract. With the emergence of the issue of "cybersecurity" in the industry and the ever-growing importance of software development for innovative fields (IoT, Industry, new mobility, etc.), the researcher wanted to concentrate on a single guide with all acceptable practices in secure software development for the industry. Our customers' feedback initiated this idea often face the choice of reference to apply and the relevance of the requirements themselves. This research is therefore intended for software architects and developers of industrial applications. It is necessary to pass it through technical and organizational measures to develop software securely. The measures and technical solutions are now numerous and continue to improve day by day. They help make life easier for developers to better prepare a deployment by improving and strengthening the verification and validation phases or exploiting a range of robust security features and mechanisms. Organizational measures will aim to create a positive and dynamic change within development teams and strengthen the product code's quality control process to improve software security level gradually. These measures include training in secure development and maintenance of the specific skills required to implement technical measures. This research aims to provide a guide to utilizing these measures, combined with the realistic acceptance criteria that suit industrial feedback.

Keywords: Cybersecurity · Development process · Security · Secure software · Best practices · Software development framework SDF

1 Introduction

Software development is now a major differentiating factor for all industries to improve software development quality for highly configurable systems. This observation can be made in several areas:

- The car, which connected vehicles have become commonplace and where manufacturers compete to offer new features to end-users;

© Springer Nature Switzerland AG 2022
D. N. A. Jawawi et al. (Eds.): ESMoC 2021, CCIS 1615, pp. 154–163, 2022.
https://doi.org/10.1007/978-3-031-19968-4_16

- Heavy industry, where production lines are becoming connected and controlled remotely, through these features directly SCADA (supervisory systems);
- Sea, where ships, but also port systems (logistics, maintenance, etc…) make calls more broadly to software to operate;

If control of software development is an asset and a significant growth driver, the problem of developing robust software from a security standpoint from Operation (SDF) and cybersecurity (and a fortiori in sectors highly constrained by regulation, as aerospace and rail) can quickly become a challenge for industrial embarking on the adventure [1].

In industry, in many aspects, the methods used for dependability fundamentally serve cybersecurity objectives. Thus, the concept of defense in depth from the SDF is perfectly applicable to the protection of face systems to computer attacks. This approach recommends the designer products (or systems) to superimpose the top protective layers, particularly around the portion which remains the most period: the software. Other activities from the safety of operation, as the search for dangerous events and analyzing preliminary hazard and risk, are all reusable elements in the field of cybersecurity [2].

2   Related Work

Traditionally, this type of security protection complements and does not directly impact the software design. It is also - for now - most often against-measures implemented at a later stage in the product design. The systems integration phase is generally the most conducive to such actions. Examples include hardening highly configurable machines, strict policy on physical and logical access control, or incoming data integrity. The ISO/IEC 27002 is a valuable aid in this field since it will list almost exhaustive so these means of protection and that, regardless of the domain for the software. But when the attacker has crossed all of these barriers, it will attempt to exploit the software's loopholes. The last defense is the strength of the software itself, and the approach is known as "Secure by Design" will try to answer it by applying the following principles:

2.1   1st Principle

Reducing the attack surface, for example, by limiting its interfaces that are internal (Bookstores, DLL…) or external (Network HMI) [3]. This measure remains the most effective and may extend to the renouncement of specific software features initially planned, but that exposes too much. One can draw a parallel with the homeless field where excessive software complexity will be banned (see rules for software development of NASA safety prescribing too many functions and SEI development rules). Cybersecurity, a "compact" software, is provided de facto fewer security holes. It is often difficult to follow, but it must be considered in the early design phases [4]. His interest is paramount since it serves both cybersecurity and the homeless.

2.2   2nd Principle

The software must integrate its defenses, such as the right to self-check to detect any loss of integrity of the executed code. Thus, in threat modeling in a distributed application, the various software modules may exchange signatures (e.g., based on a hashing function in one direction) of the executable code in a suitable challenge [5]. More typically, the exchange of data on an encrypted protocol is another example of software self-defense means. In these examples, the simplicity of interest dictated by the SDF area will be served by applying often complex cybersecurity functions. It will be necessary to weigh the risks involved in both areas and arbitrate case by case [4, 5].

2.3 3rd Principle

Confidence that is given to a software product often goes well with confidence that we will pay its development process. At this stage, Quality, homeless, and Cybersecurity will unite and agree on a common goal. Development phases must be part of a target process to minimize possible risk insertion vulnerabilities (commonly known as SDLC, Security Development Lifecycle). Here, we'll find the following development principles always well-known but alas not always applied, such as configuration management, test campaigns formwork boxes, etc. The software development process is mostly declined in standard quality or SDF (IEC 61508, DO178, ISO 26262, BV-SW100). But it will also integrate the process of developing specific phases of cybersecurity as modeling and associated flowstheir potential vulnerabilities: Spoofing, Tampering, Repudiation, Information Disclosure, Denial of Service, Elevation of Privilege (STRIDE approach from Microsoft) [6].

3 Method

The ISO/IEC 27001 and 27002, NIST, ISO 15408, ANSI/ISA 62443 (Formerly ISA99), The ISA Security Compliance Institute (ISCI) Conformity Assessment Program, ISO/IEC/IEEE 12207, Body of knowledge: SWEBOK, following various comments and feedback of experience we have had in the industrial sector, where the SDF software has already developed. It mainly addresses the principle stated above by concentrating at a reduced volume of thirty pages, acceptable practices from several secure development standards. This format facilitates its adoption by development teams already mastered the homeless but few cybersecurity [7]. This guide dedicated to Cybersecurity complements the SDF software requirements essential for building a cyber demonstration.

It is presented as a list of requirements divided into two levels: "basic" and "advanced." These levels allow modulating the approach by sector of activity, the acceptable risk level of investment possible, and vis-a-vis the effectiveness of perimeter protection layers mentioned above. How to determine and allocate security level is left free to implement this guide [8]. Each goal is associated with acceptance criteria for the evaluation of the level of coverage. This compliance with the recommendations can be made either by self or by evaluation by an external body. A certificate can be issued while valuing the effort and the costs of considering the cybersecurity approach.

3.1 V Model

The guide addresses all software development phases (cycle type V; the goals list cuts across project phases such as *System, Design, checking,* operations. To recap, the V cycle is a conceptual model of development, primarily used in software development (but, of course, applies to any development). Its name is derived from the conceptual representation of the different stages of the cycle as shown in Fig. 1:

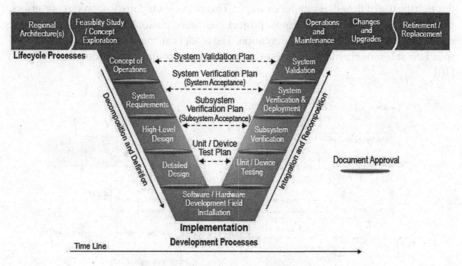

Fig. 1. Conceptual view of the V

The downward part of the cycle regarding the different expression stages needs the gathering, preparation of specifications, and refinement of the design model. In contrast, the bottom part concerns the stages of testing, verification, and validation [9]. For each of these steps, it is possible to overload them to incorporate security-related actions as in Fig. 2.

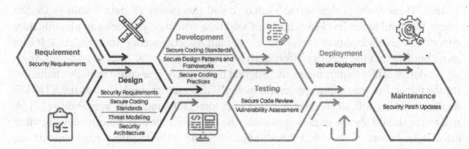

Fig. 2. Example of security processes for a software development cycle

3.2 Software Architecture

The part *System* will express requirements for upstream software development phases, for example, by asking to integrate the security perimeter identification of steps and threat modeling to derive safety requirements during the implementation phase. In this section, the focus is on the modeling of the system in its context of use (which may be in embryo on a single sheet of paper, or more formally) and the identification of the perimeter system or software component, actors (users, customer, admin) and exchanges through the use of flow diagram for example. This phase should involve product sponsors, product owners, development teams, project managers, customers, and end-users in the software, ensuring customer value creation. The model can then be refined iteratively and split into sub-models (depending on the application's complexity in question) (Fig. 3) [10].

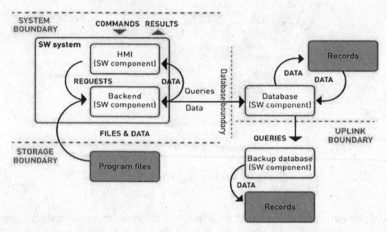

Fig. 3. An example of modeling can be a software system, identifying trusted boundary (dashed blue line)

. This modeling will allow the identification of trusted boundaries of the software system. These borders denote the exchange and processing of data within processes where the confidence level (arbitrary) of said data will change. For example, this may concern the user's inputs or exchanges via default insecure media (Internet, etc.). It is at those borders that the security effort must be worn [11].

To derive safety requirements for different flows and borders must initially characterize the threat. For this, there are several methods and metrics used, such as the STRIDE method of Microsoft, or the classic C/I/A Confidentiality, integrity, availability [12]. A risk rating should also be made to prioritize the actions needed later during development effectively. For each identified threat, objectives and testable safety requirements are formulated based on state of the art (Fig. 4) [11, 12].

3.3 Design

The part *Design* states for its part of the rules and applicable requirements during the software's design and implementation phases. These rules are the programming style used for qualification support tools through the proper use of COTS2 [13].

Boundary	Link	S	T	R	I	D	E
System	User --→HMI	X	X		X	X	
System	HMI--→ User	X	X				
Database	Backend --→ Database	X	X		X		
Database	Database --→ Backend	X	X		X		
Uplink	Database--→ Backup	X	X		X		
Storage	Program files --→ Backend	X					

Fig. 4. Example of application of the STRIDE method previously modeled system

Before the beginning of development, the team in charge must formalize the development of rules, processes, and verification tools. These rules can be purely syntactic but also binding (prohibited hazardous buildings, etc.). Many organizations, particularly in defense, automotive, or aerospace, published technical guides to serve as inspiration. We can quote the Secure Coding CERT3 -CC rules, the MISRA rules, or programming rules used at Google [14].

The qualification and the proper use of COTS are also important points to consider in software development. These are increasing, sometimes dramatically, the developed software system's attack surface and introducing vulnerabilities. Different criteria can be used to assess the relevance or not to use, as the source code's availability, project health (Active development, many contributors, monitoring and maintenance, etc.), the associated security policy, number, and track known vulnerabilities, etc. Special care should be followed to their integration, particularly in terms of security bulletins issued by CERT, to react rapidly to a new vulnerability found in a third-party component. A critical point of vigilance is emphasized in implementing security-sensitive functions such as cryptography functions if used [15]. Except for teams with established expertise in this area, today strongly advised not to implement these functions directly. Good practice would indeed turn to specialized libraries (there are for almost all languages), which have, for some of them, guarantees high security (formal evidence, external audits, etc.). These libraries typically provide APIs and clear documentation, developers offloading operations (calculated in constant time, reset the sensitive memory areas, etc.). These libraries can also be regarded as COTS in some cases. The same points of vigilance must be taken into account during their use [15, 16].

3.4 Proper Use of Tools

Today there are many tools enabling developers to write the most robust code more efficiently. It is indeed easier to correct a defect in the software during the development phase. Some tools may require some expertise to be fully exploited, and it is helpful in gradually introduce the use of new tools to avoid causing a wholesale rejection or non-use of these.

The use of tools for static code analysis (that is to say, without implementing the program), such as lenders or specific compilation passes, enables early detection of potential errors. However, these tools not all offer the same performance and guarantees (code coverage, type of errors found, completeness) Linters are the first level of a tool, easy to grip and use. They include verifying compliance with the chosen programming styles and rules and identifying trivial errors or dangerous buildings.

More elaborate, static analyzers code operate by abstract interpretation or symbolic execution are also valuable allies to highlight more subtle bugs in configurable software [17]. All analyzers do not offer the same guarantees (soundness, false positives/negatives) or even the ergonomics of use. Still, robust solutions are now available and integrated into the integration and/or continuous deployment.

The automatic prover and evidence assistants can also ensure a high level of confidence through formal methods. Their use is, however, to consider preferentially in early development or on critical portions of existing code because their implementation is more complicated than the tools mentioned above [13, 17].

3.5 Compilers Security

Modern compilers are today significant aid to the integration of security features in the generated binary. The qualification and operation of recent toolchains can provide returns on investment in terms of significant security. We can quote:

- Position Independent Executable (PIE): to take advantage of the ASLR4 security mechanism available on newer operating systems. This function allows us to load into random memory range the body of the program.
- Protection of the battery: compilers can introduce different protections to avoid crushing the stack and the function return pointer.
- Read protection only: the use of the option proceeds retro read only certain memory areas (Global Offsetle, ELF sections) can be used by an attacker to change the program execution flow.
- Integrity control flows instrumentation code at compile time to verify the execution. The control flow graph is respected. This will detect the change by an attacker place of the regular program.

However, these features are not without consequences on code size or execution speed [18].

3.6 Console Code at Compile

Besides adding security features cheaply, modern compilers can also significantly help developers instrument their code to identify more efficient and faster software defects during test phases. In this context, a series of functions, called Sanitizers, was added in recent years to market-leading compilers (GCC and Clang, particular). However, their use is imperative reserved for test builds because their cost in terms of performance is prohibitive in production. An attacker can exploit the information provided during a crash to exploit a software weakness. The interest in sanitizers becomes apparent when combined with automated testing tools (fuzzing) adequate code coverage during the verification and validation phases. Indeed, sanitizers will increase code coverage of fuzzing tools and generate more detailed crash reports on the bug's origin (memory addresses involved, etc.) [19].

3.7 Verification and Validation

The part *checking* focuses on the safety requirements for the test and validation phases of V's cycle. Among these, we can state for known vulnerabilities, such as CWE5 and CVE6, within the software and its dependencies (libraries software, external binary). It is also recommended to perform penetration testing or fuzzing tests on the product to verify the implemented security features [20].

The interest of verification tools and automated testing is here to emphasize, especially on codebases whose size prevents them from helpful, comprehensive manual reviews. They also will potentially detect bugs or security flaws in some functions used or little stressed at runtime.

3.8 Exploitation and Maintaining Safe Condition

The part *operations* regarding the initial operation phase and operating software, with requirements for the standby vulnerabilities external dependencies involved in a security function (for example, monitoring security vulnerabilities Open SSL for cryptographic mechanisms) and updating security incidents [21]. Telemetry implemented in software can allow studying the use or misuse of internal protection mechanisms and good security posture layout incidents (fallback or fail-safe). Similarly, and on specific security configuration documentation, a return process to the default settings can also be provided. An update procedure must also be defined and carried securely with verification of the patches' integrity [19, 21].

4 Discussion

Software lifecycle is a key to successful development. Secure development is only possible if the cycle is compact and modeled effectively. In simple words, it is the energy fluid of software development. Anyone can understand the maturity level of any product or an organization by looking at its development cycle. Secure software development practices four things to make it compact and vigilant which are: Organizational preparation. Things to focus on for software protection, the procedure used for secure development, and first thing respond to any vulnerability. Security issues of software development are multi-directional or multi-dimensional, which must be addressed during the development life cycle. In the future, companies adopt these considerations to particular the security and the effective building of software without any ambiguity or loophole.

5 Conclusion

We have seen in this article, to develop software securely, it is necessary to pass it through technical and organizational measures. The measures and technical solutions are now numerous and continue to improve day by day. They help make life easier for developers to better prepare a deployment by improving and strengthening the verification and validation phases or to exploit a range of robust security features and mechanisms efficiently. Organizational measures will aim to create a positive and dynamic change within development teams and gradually strengthen the product code's quality control process to gradually improve the software security level. In particular, these measures include training in secure development and maintenance of the specific skills required to implement technical measures. This research aims to provide a guide to utilizing these measures, combined with the realistic acceptance criteria that suit industrial feedback.

References

1. Ali, A., Hafeez, Y., Hussain, S., Yang, S.: Role of requirement prioritization technique to improve the quality of highly-configurable systems. IEEE Access **8**, 2754927573 (2020)
2. Borsukovskyi, Y.: Defining requirements to develop information security concept N hybrid threats conditions. Part 2. Cybersecurity, Educ., Sci., Tech. **2**(6), 112121 (2019). https://doi.org/10.28925/2663-4023.2019.6.112121
3. Changazi, S.A., Shafi, I., Saleh, K., Islam, M.H., Hussainn, S.M., Ali, A.: Performance enhancement of snort IDS through kernel modification. In: 2019 8th International Conference on Information and Communication Technologies (ICICT), pp. 155–161. IEEE (2019)
4. Ali, A., Hafeez, Y., Abbas, S.F., Sarwar, A.: Requirements prioritization: a comparison between traditional and agile (SCRUM AND FDD). In: 16th International Conference on Statistical Sciences, p. 77 (2018)
5. Hussain, S.M., Islam, M.H., Ali, A., Nazir, M.U.: Threat modeling framework for security of unified storages in private data centers. In: 2020 IEEE 22nd Conference on Business Informatics (CBI), vol. 2, pp. 111–120. IEEE (2020)
6. Alenezi, M., Almuairfi, S.: Security risks in the software development lifecycle. Int. J. Recent Technol. Eng. **8**(3), 7048–7055 (2019). https://doi.org/10.35940/ijrte.C5374.098319
7. Dotsenko, S., Illiashenko, O., Kamenskyi, S., Kharchenko, V.: Integrated model of knowledge management for security of information technologies: standards ISO/IEC 15408 and ISO/IEC 18045. Inform. Secur.: an Int. J. **43**(3), 305317 (2019). https://doi.org/10.11610/isij.4323
8. Brottier, E., Le Traon, Y., Nicolas, B.: Composing models at two modeling levels to capture heterogeneous concerns in requirements. In: Baudry, B., Wohlstadter, E. (eds.) SC 2010. LNCS, vol. 6144, pp. 1–16. Springer, Heidelberg (2010). https://doi.org/10.1007/978-3-642-14046-4_1
9. Essebaa, I., Chantit, S.: A combination of V development life cycle and modelbased testing to deal with software system evolution issues. In: Proceedings of the 6th International Conference on Model-Driven Engineering and Software Development (2018). https://doi.org/10.5220/0006657805280535
10. Kneuper, R.: Translating data protection into software requirements. In: Proceedings of the 6th International Conference on Information Systems Security and Privacy (2020). https://doi.org/10.5220/0008873902570264
11. Zhang, N., Liu, Z., Han, H.: Big data privacy protection model based on multi-level trusted system. In: AIP Conference Proceedings, vol. 1967, p. 040014 (2018). https://doi.org/10.1063/1.5039088
12. Al-Far, A., Qusef, A., Almajali, S.: Measuring impact score on confidentiality, integrity, and availability using code metrics. In: 2018 International Arab Conference on Information Technology (ACIT) (2018). https://doi.org/10.1109/acit.2018.8672678
13. Holtkamp, P., Jokinen, J.P., Pawlowski, J.M.: Soft competency requirements in requirements engineering, software design, implementation, and testing. J. Syst. Softw. **101**, 136–146 (2015). https://doi.org/10.1016/j.jss.2014.12.010
14. Karniel, A., Reich, Y.: Interpretation using implementation rules and business rules. In: Managing the Dynamics of New Product Development Processes, pp. 153–168 (2011). https://doi.org/10.1007/978-0-85729-570-5_10

15. Fox, G., Lantner, K., Marcom, S.: A software development process for COTS-based information system infrastructure. In: Proceedings Fifth International Symposium on Assessment of Software Tools and Technologies, pp. 133–142 (1997). https://doi.org/10.1109/AST.1997.599923

16. Kumar, A., Jain, M.: Using ensemble learning libraries. In: Ensemble Learning for AI Developers, pp. 61–96. Apress, Berkeley, CA (2020). https://doi.org/10.1007/978-1-4842-5940-5_5

17. Ali, A., Hafeez, Y., Hussainn, S.M., Nazir, M.U.: BIO-Inspired communication: a review on solution of complex problems for highly configurable systems. In: 2020 3rd International Conference on Computing, Mathematics and Engineering Technologies (iCoMET), pp. 1–6. IEEE (2020)

18. Bresson, E., Manulis, M., Schwenk, J.: On security models and compilers for group key exchange protocols. In: Miyaji, A., Kikuchi, H., Rannenberg, K. (eds.) IWSEC 2007. LNCS, vol. 4752, pp. 292–307. Springer, Heidelberg (2007). https://doi.org/10.1007/978-3-540-75651-4_20

19. Damevski, K., Shepherd, D., Pollock, L.: A field study of how developers locate features in source code. Empir. Softw. Eng. **21**(2), 724–747 (2015). https://doi.org/10.1007/s10664-015-9373-9

20. Petrenko, A.: Checking experiments for symbolic input/Output finite state machines. In: 2016 IEEE Ninth International Conference on Software Testing, Verification and Validation Workshops (ICSTW) (2016). https://doi.org/10.1109/icstw.2016.9

21. Held, G.: Overcoming wireless LAN security vulnerabilities. In: Tipton, H., Tipton, H.F., Krause, M. (eds.) Information Security Management: Handbook, Vol. 4, pp. 167–174. Auerbach Publications (2019). https://doi.org/10.1201/9781351073547-13

A Survey on Measurement Based Shadow Fading Model for Vehicular Communications

Tahir Iqbal[1], Muhammad Bilal[2], Asif Farooq[3], Nadeem Sarwar[1(✉)],
Asghar Ali Shah[1], and Taimoor Aamer Chughtai[1]

[1] Department of Computer Science, Bahria University Lahore Campus, Lahore, Pakistan
tahir.iqbal@bahria.edu.pk, Nadeem_srwr@yahoo.com
[2] Department of Electrical Engineering, Air University Islamabad, Islamabad, Pakistan
mbilal@mail.au.edu.pk
[3] Department of Computer Science, University of Lahore, Lahore, Pakistan
asif.farooq@cs.uol.edu.pk

Abstract. With advancement in technology and research in 5G and higher frequency bands we are going to automate our transportation systems by using such high frequency in which the vehicles will not only communicate with other vehicle. But the current cellular network channel models cannot be applied here as the vehicles, transmitter and receiver, are mobile. ALSO, the signal will be greatly affected by the shadowing and fading phenomenon. So, there is need of separate channel model that will cater the losses in V2V communications. In this paper a detail research work has been presented in which researchers tried to find the characteristics of the channel using certain scenarios like rural, urban, highway and on motorways. The data was measured and then simulated and found the desired results about the channel modelling.

Keywords: V2V · LOS · OLOS · NLOS · Channel modelling · Shadowing · Fading · VANETS

1 Introduction

Vehicle to vehicle to communication plays an important part in the today's world. Vehicles will communicate with each other for safer journey and collision between vehicles can be greatly decreased. But it is typically different than current cellular networks as it will be based on adhoc topology, both the vehicles, Tx and Rx will be mobile [1] and there will great loss of signal strength as frequency is higher than current cellular systems.

A number of experiments have performed to find the channel statistics for V2V communication as there are three major factors that affect the efficiency of V2V communication these are path losses, attenuation and fading of signals [2]. As Tx and Rx both are mobile also there will be buildings and other scatters around them, signal will pass through multiple path and will be degraded, so all these need careful attention to be find before modeling a channel for V2V communication.

© Springer Nature Switzerland AG 2022
D. N. A. Jawawi et al. (Eds.): ESMoC 2021, CCIS 1615, pp. 164–172, 2022.
https://doi.org/10.1007/978-3-031-19968-4_17

There is LOS; NLOS and OLOS paths which signals will follow to reach the Rx. LOS is [3] the signal with less fading as directly received without any reflection. NLOS is received through multiple paths with severe fading and sometimes is greater power as multiple copies are received through different paths and gain is achieved. OLOS is due to the vehicle running on the roads to Tx and Rx. They will cause a blockade to the signals.

Previous models are specific to cellular communication. These were indoor and outdoor propagation models that describe the propagation of wave when it passes through environment and causes certain attenuation offered by the environment and surrounding obstacles. As Vehicular communication is little bit different than cellular communication as both the transmitter and receiver both are mobile. There is no concept of fixed base station, so a need of new channel model is need for such communication as the previous one cannot be applied to mv2v communication.

2 Literature Review

A. Path Models

1- Free Space Model

In this model, it is assumed that there is no obstruction to the signal so signal follows LOS. But the distance between transmitter and receiver is very important for the received signal at receiver.

The Friis equation [4] for free space model is:

$$\Pr(d) = P_t G_t G_r \left(\frac{\lambda}{4\pi d}\right)^2 \tag{1}$$

where Pt is power of transmitting antenna, Gt, Gr define gains for transmitting antenna and receiver antenna respectively.

λ defines the wavelength of operating frequency and d shows the distance between receiver & transmitter.

2- Two Ray Model

This model is assumed to be the simplest path loss model as it considers signals from both the direct as well as reflected path.

$$\text{Equation is: } pr = pt*Gt*Gr*\left(\frac{ht*hr}{d^2}\right)^2 \tag{2}$$

Transmitter height is represented by 'ht', while height of receiver is shown by 'hr]. Distance between Tx & Rx shown by 'd', while 'Pt' shows power of transmitter while Gt, Gr here represents the gain of Tx and Rx. While Rx power is shown by pr. This model is used if the distance of transmitting device and receiving device is much greater than the transmitting device height and the height of receiving device.

3- Okumura Model

This model is widely applicable for urban areas for signal detection. This model is working on up to 1950 MHz. And distance of up to 100 km. This model is widely used in cellular systems for the predictions of loss in environment. It is one of the simplest models. But this model does not fit well when there is fast changing/sped of the vehicle in the area. Also not well for rural areas.

4- HATA Model

The extension to the above model is provided by HATA. In this model graphical formulations were provided for the data to calculate the path loss. It works well for up to 1500 MHz. It gives the same results as given by okumura. This model is well suited for large scale signal propagation in cellular systems.

5- Cost231 Model

When it comes to the path loss propagation the one of the best model is provided by this one, as this is well suited for wireless mobile systems. It is suited for mostly all types of environment like urban, sub urban etc.

B. Related Work

Taimoor Abbas, [1] Katrin Sjoberg et al. [5] performed some experiment in Sweden to find the performance of channel for v2v communication. In this work they presented the effect of shadow fading. They measured the data on urban and suburban highways. The measured data was separated according to LOS, NLOS, and OLOS. The OLOS due to other vehicles on the road provide additional fading to the signal of about 10db at receiver Fig. 1 and 2.

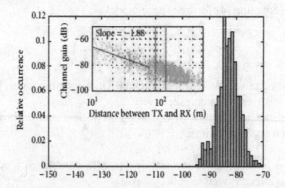

Fig. 1. Channel gain for suburban highways

In their work they eliminated the effect of small scale fading as they took average the of power which was received at the receiver for a distance of 15 λ. So, the affect seen in envelop was due to the large scale fading caused by shadowing, other vehicles and nearby buildings. So, they focused to model the large-scale effect on the signal. Approach used to model was log normal distribution.

In 2010, J. Gozalvez and Miguel Sepulcre presented a paper [1] in which they tried to design a protocol for efficient v2v communication. Their main aim is to design radio

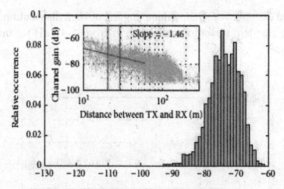

Fig. 2. Channel gain for urban highways

channel for safety application in v2v. As antenna heights are very lower and the network changes its topology in v2v very fast because mobility of receiver & transmitter. So, these alterations can affect the performance of the protocols. They used path models of free space and for higher losses such as in urban environment used a model called 'logdistance path loss'.

$$PL(d) = PL(d_0) + 10*n*\log_{10}\left(\frac{d}{d_0}\right) \tag{3}$$

where small 'n' shows an exponent for path loss, which depends upon the environment; PL (do) shows the loss of power at distance do.

Normally the n value ranges from 2.7–5 for urban environment and for free space it is chosen as n = 2. One issue in the above two models are they result same for the LOS and NLOS scenario. So, they used a new model that would use both LOS/NLOS scenarios. The result of the model is shown below in Fig. 3.

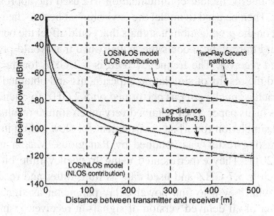

Fig. 3. Received power level for various path loss

They modeled the effect of shadowing using log normal distribution. For log normal mean is zero and standard deviation value ranges from 4–12 dB for outdoor shown in Fig. 4.

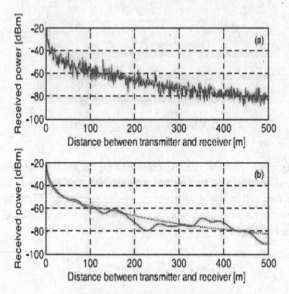

Fig. 4. Shadowing effect

So, their work greatly influences the researchers to implement such channel models that should not affect the performance and working of protocols used in v2v as for safety vehicles.

In 2004, W. Wiesbeck published his work [6] where they presented to introduce a new channel model for inter vehicular communication. He used the approach to design the traffic on the road. Then he used to model the environment near to the road as it has also significant impact on the propagation of signals that could affect the performance of v2v communication and thirdly, he models the actual wave that would propagate between the transmitter and receiver. The frequency used is 5.2 GHZ for the communication. Then he compared the results of simulation experiments and obtained the almost same results. His approach is much better as performed on 5.2 GHZ frequency, but he did not consider protocols in his paper. They obtained very much similar results when compared measurement and simulation for urban environment for slow fading in Fig. 5.

Another interesting result was obtained by Panagiotis, Mahler et al. When they published [7] in 2011. They experimented using frequency little bit higher than the previous one which is 5.7 GHZ and used cars as transmitter and receivers to find the path loss. Along with they also find power delay parameter as signals follow NLOS so calculated power of all delayed version of signals at receiver. Using four modeling approaches, they find the power decay for multipath and path loss.

Specifically, for OLOS [8], which is taken as truck that can affect the communication of V2V was experimented by Dimitrios Vlastaras*, Taimoor Abbas et al. As so far, we are

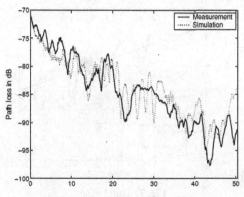

Fig. 5. Slow fading (Time in Sec)

quite understand that shadowing affect the signals strength in Fig. 6. So the authors now tried to impose the same phenomenon on v2v communication using truck as shadowing obstacle. And then find and characterize the channel model. Using roof antenna on vehicle they found the obstacle truck reduce the signals strength on average of 10–13 db. This value is for rural and highways respectively when the all are in motion. Also, the truck obstructed the LOS between transmitter and receiver vehicle.

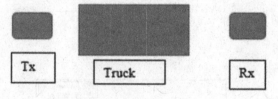

Fig. 6. OLOS scenario

They noticed that the power at receiver is less when it is nearer to the OLOS truck, and found that it is better when OLOS truck is at some distance. Which shows path loss exponent is low for OLOS cases. They also found one more result that when on highways, gain was higher in OLOS case as compared to the rural shown in Fig. 7 and 8. This was found because in there is more scatters in rural as is on a highway in which only OLOS cause a signal to block but in rural there are bridges, pulls trees etc. from these multipath signals arrives at receiver so cause greatly fading. The results are shown below.

They also presented the loss due to shadowing which is dependent on the separation and distance of two, transmitting vehicle and the vehicle that received, so subtracted measured mean pth loss of LOS from OLOS data. Result is below in Fig. 9.

So this was the first work done by others using truck as OLOS and measured the path loss parameters, that results help in modeling a channel in inter vehicular communication. But these results were specific to a certain area; other location may have some different results.

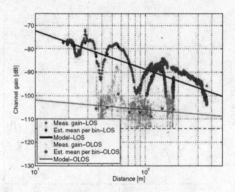

Fig. 7. Rural case

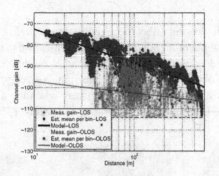

Fig. 8. Highway case

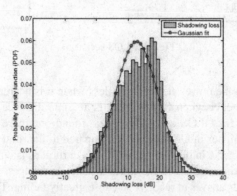

Fig. 9. Shadowing loss due to truck

A paper [9] discussed path loss characteristics of Vehicular communication using 5.9 GHZ frequency for both LOS and NLOS. They found path loss in 03 separate conditions; one is urban having less flow of traffic, second is urban with average traffic and third is on high-speed road. The values from path loss were found from the above scenarios and will be used to design vehicular networks using VANETS simulators for future work. Some of the results are presented below in Fig. 10.

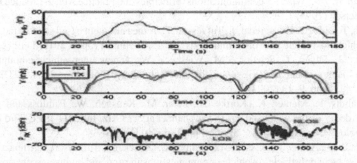

Fig. 10. a-Transmitter-receiver distance, b-Vehicles speed, c-Power received

It can be easily stated from the figure above that LOS has little variation in received power as LOS has dominant signal while NLOS [10] has higher fluctuation due to multipath and changes with time and speed of vehicle.

3 Discussion and Conclusion

We have surveyed the work and critically analysed the previous work for vehicular communications and adopted the conclusion that no single model is catering the need for path loss in vehicular communization as environment changes the path model under experiment does not give suit results as environment has been changed. So a new model is needed for this type of communications to measure the path loss. Different experiments were performed under different scenarios but model was changed in each experiment and analysed different results. From all the above discussed work, we noticed that each paper is specific to some problem, some discussed for urban environment other discussed rural and highways. Losses can be seen from the results as in V2V due to shadowing etc. Results showed that they greatly matched with the simulated results but the problem is that experiments were specific to some country and locality it will be different from country to country as the topology and environment changes. So still there is much opportunity to work on the topic for different scenarios and then come out for a channel model for vehicular communication which will improve the safety of the vehicles. So we critically analyze the previous works and extract that we need a new model for vehicular communications that will be acceptable in all types, countries, topologies and in different scenarios will work.

References

1. Gozalvez, J., Sepulcre, M., Bauza, R.: Impact of the radio channel modelling on the performance of VANET communication protocols. Telecommun. Syst. **50**(3), 149–167 (2012)
2. Molisch, A.: Wireless Communications. IEEE Press-Wiley, Chichester, UK (2005)

3. Abbas, T., Karedal, J., Tufvesson, F., Paier, A., Bernad´o, L., Molisch, A.F.: Directional analysis of vehicle-to-vehicle propagation channels. In: Proceedings of the IEEE 73rd Vehicular Technology Conference (VTC-Spring'11), pp. 1–5 (2011)
4. Rappaport, T.S.: Wireless communications: principles and practice, vol. 2. Prentice Hall PTR, New Jersey (1996)
5. Abbas, T., Sjöberg, K., Karedal, J., Tufvesson, F.: A measurement based shadow fading model for vehicle-to-vehicle network simulations. Int. J. Antennas Propag. **2015**, 1–12 (2015)
6. Maurer, J., Fugen, T., Schafer, T.M., Wiesbeck, W.: A new inter-vehicle communications (IVC) channel model. In: IEEE 60th Vehicular Technology Conference, 2004. VTC2004-Fall. 2004, vol. 1, pp. 9–13 (2004)
7. Paschalidis, P., Mahler, K., Kortke, A., Peter, M., Keusgen, W.: Pathloss and multipath power decay of the wideband car-to-car channel at 5.7 GHz. In: 2011 IEEE 73rd Vehicular Technology Conference (VTC Spring), pp. 1–5 (2011)
8. Vlastaras, D., Abbas, T., Nilsson, M., Whiton, R., Olback, M., Tufvesson, F.: Impact of a truck as an obstacle on vehicle-tovehicle communications in rural and highway scenarios. In: Proceedings of the IEEE 6th International Symposium on Wireless Vehicular Communications (WiVeC'14), pp. 1–6. Vancouver, Canada (2014)
9. Fernández, H., Rodrigo-Peñarrocha, V.M., Rubio, L., Reig, J.: Path loss characterization in vehicular environments under LOS and NLOS conditions at 5.9 GHz. In: The 8th European Conference on Antennas and Propagation (EuCAP 2014), pp. 3044–3048 (2014)
10. Samimi, M.K., Rappaport, T.S.: Ultra-wideband statistical channel model for non line of sight millimeter-wave urban channels. In: 2014 IEEE Global Communications Conference (GLOBECOM), pp. 3483–3489 (2014)

Author Index

Printed in the United States
by Baker & Taylor Publisher Services